"Elizabeth Benedict's magical mystery tour of sex between the pages manages at once to be instructive, entertaining, and literary. She gives the term 'word play' new meaning."

—MICHAEL DORRIS

"*The Joy of Writing Sex* isn't so much an instruction manual on how to do this as it is a license to go ahead and try, with a wealth of suggestions for how to approach the task."

—*The Women's Review of Books*

"I used to have straight hair before I read this book. And I never had hair on my chest! *The Joy of Writing Sex* carries bracing doses of testosterone, progesterone, estrogen, and musk. A wonderful and handy compendium of how to write—and have fun with—sex."

—CAROLYN SEE

"Despite its sense of fun, this volume is far more substantive than most how-to-write manuals and is certain to be of interest to aspiring writers of literary fiction."

—*Booklist*

"Elizabeth Benedict's advice for writers about the literary meaning of sex is also wonderful advice for readers. An important book for all serious teachers and students of contemporary fiction."

—ELAINE SHOWALTER

"All our writing students will henceforth find in their information packets the recommendation that they read the new *Joy of Writing Sex*. . . . The new edition is broader, its brief interview with a variety of novelists lively, suggestive, and occasionally hilarious. The wit and cunning of Benedict's writing are every bit as impressive as they were in the remarkable original book."

—ROBERT BOYERS,
director, New York State Summer Writers Institute

Almost
Safe Conduct
The Beginner's Book of Dreams
Slow Dancing

THE JOY OF

WRITING

SEX

THE JOY OF WRITING SEX

A GUIDE FOR

FICTION WRITERS

Revised and Updated

ELIZABETH BENEDICT

A HOLT PAPERBACK

Henry Holt and Company   New York

Holt Paperbacks
Henry Holt and Company, LLC
Publishers since 1866
175 Fifth Avenue
New York, New York 10010
www.henryholt.com

Library of Congress Cataloging-in-Publication Data
Benedict, Elizabeth.
  The joy of writing sex: a guide for fiction writers/Elizabeth Benedict.
    p.   cm.
  Includes index.
  ISBN-13: 978-0-8050-6993-8
  ISBN-10: 0-8050-6993-3
    1. Erotic stories—Authorship. I. Title.
PN 3377.5.E76 B46 2002
808.3'85—dc21

                                                      2001039839

First Edition 2002

Printed in the United States of America

P1

This is for
JEROME BADANES
(1937–1995),
who taught me that sometimes
it has to be over the top
to be in the right place,
and for
LEE GOERNER
(1947–1995),
who cared about every last word.

It is a bawdy planet.

—SHAKESPEARE,
The Winter's Tale

Sex does not thrive on monotony. Without feelings, inventions, moods, [there are] no surprises in bed. Sex must be mixed with tears, laughter, words, promises, scenes, jealousy, envy, all the spices of fear, foreign travel, new faces, novels, stories, dreams, fantasies, music, dancing, opium, wine.

—ANAÏS NIN,
from a letter, reprinted in her
diary, to the man paying her
one dollar a page to write
erotic stories

Anyone who attempts to render sexual experience directly must face the fact that the writhings which comprise it are ludicrous without their subjective content.

—WILLIAM GASS,
On Being Blue

CONTENTS

Preface
to the Revised Edition

Sex matters.

In the six years since I wrote the original *Joy of Writing Sex*, in 1995, the extent to which it matters in real life, in our private and public lives, has been proven more often than necessary to make the point.

It matters—but has it *changed* in the last six years?

In a word, yes.

Make that three words: Cyberspace. Monica. AIDS.

For many of us individually and for the culture as a whole, each of these phenomena has altered the ways we define, communicate, negotiate, and even experience sex, so much so that the editors and I felt it was time to take a fresh look at how these changes have filtered down into the fiction we read and write.

In today's fiction, it's almost as common to find references to e-mail and the Internet as to the telephone. Flirtation, romantic connections, and sexual stimulation are familiar cyber-occurrences in literature, as in life. The eighteenth-century epistolary novel— *Les Liaisons Dangereuses, Clarissa, Pamela*—finds its contemporary echo in Matt Beaumont's comic *e: A Novel,* which is told entirely in e-mail messages that circulate among staffers in a London advertising agency.

In our long association with AIDS, it has now become routine for even the most bourgeois heterosexual fictional characters to carry condoms and to have "the talk" before falling into bed together, a pronounced change from the fiction I read six and seven years ago, where the subject was more often ignored. For homosexual characters, "the talk" and the context are much more complicated, in ways we'll look at in chapter 4.

Lastly, there is what I call the "Monica effect." I don't mean that Ms. Lewinsky has become a popular fictional motif, though Philip Roth set his recent novel, *The Human Stain,* in the summer of the Clinton impeachment hearings and makes her a subject of some interest, as does John Updike in "Rabbit Remembered." Francine Prose, in her novel *Blue Angel,* indirectly satirizes Special Prosecutor Kenneth Starr's sexual witch-hunt. More generally, I mean by the "Monica effect" that two solid years of the psychic and linguistic challenges of discussing the president's sex life on *Meet the Press* and ABC's *World News Tonight,* as well as with curious young children and befuddled senior citizens, have forced us to loosen up and have seriously shifted the standards for what we can talk about at dinner parties and in casual conversations. The experience of reading the Starr Report in the *New York Times* was a cultural watershed; now that all those sexual details have been spelled out in the nation's paper of record, none of us can claim innocence any longer. We are certainly no longer innocent of the lengths to which some people go to meet their sexual needs and others go to expose and exploit them for political gain—and how much all of this can cost, in dollars and everything else that matters. In our age of memoir, confession, and reality TV, the personal is political—or at least it is no longer private.

Thirty years ago, Philip Roth's writing about Alex Portnoy masturbating with a piece of raw liver sent shock waves through the literary world and beyond. In a sly acknowledgment of that literary watershed, Francine Prose opened *Blue Angel* with a creative writing professor conducting a classroom discussion about a student's short story in which a teenage boy "rapes an uncooked chicken by the light of the family fridge."

Sex still matters, and any way you look at it, we are not in Kansas anymore.

With these attitudinal changes in mind—and in evidence in our recent fiction—I set out to revise and update *The Joy of Writing Sex*. I have been fortunate enough to conduct new interviews with Edmund White, Charles Baxter, and Darin Strauss, whose celebrated first novel, *Chang and Eng*, published in 2000, includes imagined sex scenes of the original Siamese twins with their wives. I have written a new chapter on intimacy on the Internet; a new chapter about wedding nights and honeymoons, because I have found so many wonderful examples in recent fiction; and I have added a chapter about AIDS awareness in fiction in 2001, which now prefaces the original AIDS chapter, written in 1995. It's also been my pleasure to add examples from some notable pieces of recent fiction, passages that are funny, smart, original, psychologically and linguistically rich, or all of the above.

In reading for the revision, I have been impressed to find so many men and women writing smashingly well about sex, about its pleasures, burdens, consequences, and mysteries. The new examples I've selected are by writers from the United States, England, Ireland, and India; they don't begin to suggest the number I had to choose from. Every week seems to bring a new novel or collection of stories that someone tells me I should read, and I am torn, even as we go to press, between reading more and meeting my deadline. My apologies to those I could not include.

THE JOY OF

WRITING

SEX

INTRODUCTION:
WHY SEX IN FICTION IS
SO DIFFICULT TO WRITE

Sexual explicitness in fiction these days is so much a part of the literary landscape that there is even a Bad Sex Award given every year in England by Auberon Waugh's magazine, *The Literary Review.* Intended to shame serious writers, not pornographers, into improving their sex scenes, the prize money is given not to the writer but to the reader who located the offending passage. The "winning" writer receives an embarrassing sculpture and the obligation to give an acceptance speech at the awards ceremony.

Writing fiction about sex in our culture has always been tricky—and still is, even with all the freedom of expression we now have. By and large, we are afflicted with a multiple personality disorder: We are sex-crazed Puritans, scandalized by President Clinton's indiscretions but eager to read, while waiting on the supermarket checkout line, the women's magazine article entitled "Twelve Dirty Words That'll Drive Your Man Wild." Twenty million people a year visit Las Vegas, where strip shows and "exotic dancers" who make house calls are as plentiful as slot machines, but we elect neighbors to school boards who will ban Toni Morrison's novels from the high school library. Men, women, and children are bombarded hourly with pornography on our computers, much of it via e-mail, unsolicited ("Teen Sluts Like Anal Sex," I read one morning in my inbox), but in many school districts, sex education classes are as popular as needle exchange programs. In Georgia, Alabama, and Texas, it's illegal to own a vibrator but not a gun.

The truth is that different populations, religions, and interest groups have different values—and many of us are full of internal erotic conflict, engaged in a struggle between what we desire and what is permissible or possible. A snapshot of the culture at this moment suggests that we want it all: sex, titillation, true love, and family values.

Not surprisingly, with messages as mixed as these, when we sit down to write a sex scene, our circuits can jam, our feelings of self-consciousness surge, and we might as well be beginning students of English as a second language. How do you create a sex scene now that "the language of sensuality has become so eroded by popular culture," as novelist Carol Shields wrote in a letter to me. For some of us, the challenges are about language and literary choices. How explicit should I be? What do I call this and that? For other writers, anxiety, embarrassment, even shame seize control of our creative energies—because even with all of our freedoms, we are still creatures of our families, our histories, and the real worlds in which we live.

We may not want our spouses, lovers, or children to know where our sexual fantasies take us. The eloquent observations Georges Bataille made in 1957, in the classic *Eroticism: Death and Sensuality,* are hauntingly true forty years later: "The human spirit is prey to the most astounding impulses. Man goes constantly in fear of himself. His erotic urges terrify him. The saint turns from the voluptuary in alarm; she does not know that his unacknowledgeable passions and her own are really one." Our sexual urges and behavior are complicated; so are society's responses to them.

The Joy of Writing Sex is intended to help you make sense of this territory as it relates to writing fiction.

My aim is only to help writers craft better sex scenes. I don't have any other agenda. That is to say, I don't believe sex scenes are necessary in fiction. I don't believe that more sex scenes are better than fewer, nor that sex scenes should be long, elaborate, or explicit—*unless* that is what the work and the moment call for. I believe it is foolish to prohibit people from writing about sex, and unfortunate when people *feel* prohibited, whether they fear the long arm of the law, the ghost of a grandmother, the remembered wrath of a religious authority, or the day-to-day insecurities of the man or woman they live with. My primary allegiance as a writer, reader, and teacher is to good prose, whether the subject is sex, sainthood, or circumnavigation. The only sin I recognize is writing that is imprecise, flabby, sentimental, or fundamentally dishonest about the experience of being human.

As we embark on the process of learning to write well about sex in fiction, we need to remember that the sexual tenor of the time, place, and family in which we grew up is marked indelibly on our psyches. Whether we embrace it or struggle mightily to reject it, when we turn our energies to writing fiction, it travels with us.

Before you turn your attention to the body of this book, take some time to reflect on the sexual attitudes of the family and culture in which you were raised. Free-associate with pen in hand or sitting at the computer. You might unearth material or gain insight into what makes you and your characters tick when the narrative veers in the direction of the bedroom. Novelist Stephen Harrigan told me that "the abhorrence of sex," drilled into him by his education in Catholic schools in the 1950s, makes writing every sex scene for him "a declaration of independence." Though he was raised to believe he would burn in hell for having impure thoughts, it's his job to have them, he says, "and it's worth risking going to hell to get the scene right."

For myself, I was given permission to write about sex in my fiction long before I knew how badly I would need it. In my sophomore year at Barnard College, three graduates returned one afternoon to tell us about their careers as writers. They spoke in a science lecture hall with the periodic table of elements hanging behind them. I sat in the front row, hanging on to their every word; I already knew I wanted to do what they did. One writer was a perky, blond-haired poet with a Chinese name, class of '63, whose first novel was about to be published. I don't remember much of what she said that day in 1973, but of course I remember her name. Erica Jong.

Several months later, *Fear of Flying* erupted into all of our lives. On every page, Jong's saucy heroine, Isadora Wing, celebrated orgasms, infidelity, masturbation, and something truly revolutionary called "the zipless fuck," which happened when you met a man on a train, had sex with him *right there*, and never saw him again—or even wanted to! That women, nice girls with college degrees, thought these things, did these things, and *said* them in print—today it is impossible to convey how mind-boggling a notion this was for those of us raised, not so long ago, believing we would be virgins when we got married.

At nineteen, I didn't know enough about sex or writing to do much with the freedoms that were now mine for the taking, but I knew something had changed. I knew to pay attention to the uproar and upheaval that Jong and the women's movement had ignited. I knew there was something in it for me as a woman, and as an aspiring writer.

Women's rights and women's sexual pleasure were now front-page news, the nitty-gritty details debated passionately and publicly. The female orgasm had become the symbol and substance of who controlled language, women's bodies, and, as it turned out, everything else. In books, broadsides, and the pages of a new magazine called *Ms.*, we pondered and practiced real orgasms versus fake, clitoral versus vaginal, Freud versus Masters and Johnson. Dr. Freud lost a lot of standing in this debate for having claimed that a clitoral orgasm was "immature" and a vaginal orgasm was "mature," but the reputation of the Greek sage Tiresias was burnished. Having been both man and woman, he was asked by the gods which gender enjoyed sex more. He told them that women got nine times more pleasure than men and was promptly blinded for his trouble. His candor was not much more welcome in Puritan North America, until Isadora Wing admitted to us how she could "come and come and come."

Once I started to write seriously, in my early twenties, it never occurred to me *not* to write about sex, any more than it would have occurred to the Romantics not to write about Grecian urns, churchyards, or nightingales. And it never occurred to me that I would not be permitted to say whatever I pleased. But of course the thaw had been a long time coming. It was not until the 1960s that most of us could write explicitly without the threat of censorship, without the trials, jail sentences, bannings, confiscated books, and the incalculable tragedies of self-censorship and silence. It was not until then that writers could abandon the vagueness, codings, and tortured indirection that even the best resorted to when they knew that plain speaking might force them into exile or land them behind bars.

The subject of censorship is a book, or a library of books. As a place to begin, I recommend *Girls Lean Back Everywhere: The Law of Obscenity and the Assault on Genius* by Edward de Grazia (Vintage paperback). It is a lively, comprehensive oral history of literary censorship told by banned authors, their publishers, and the lawyers who defended them.

WHAT THIS BOOK IS AND ISN'T

The Joy of Writing Sex aims to help you write well about sex in fiction that is about something other than the mechanics of sex, whether the sex is great, obligatory, or unwelcome; whether it fizzles, makes you laugh, flinch, or weep. It is not a primer for

writing pornography and not a collection of tips on how to write
erotically charged sex scenes.

As near as I can define it, the difference between pornographic
writing—which Edmund White, in our recent interview, catego-
rized as a form of sex—and the kind of sex writing I focus on here
is that to the extent you remember anything when pornography is
over, you remember the intensity of the orgasms the otherwise
unmemorable characters had, or you had. In pornography, con-
sumers will demand their money back if the sex is lousy (i.e., the
guy doesn't come) or the girl cries when it's over. This other kind
of sex writing thrives on all the things that nourish good fiction:
tension, dramatic conflict, character development, insights, metaphors, and surprises.

As with all good fiction writing, and all good sex, there are no
rules or formulas for exactly what to do and how to do it, no
recipes that guarantee your soufflé will rise every time. What I
offer here instead is a comprehensive way of thinking about and
reading sex scenes culled from my twenty years of writing novels
and short stories, fifteen years of teaching fiction writing, and
from reading many stacks of excellent fiction.

My four organizing principles are these:

1. A good sex scene is not always about good sex but it is always
   an example of good writing.
2. A good sex scene should always connect to the larger concerns of the work.
3. The needs, impulses, and histories of your characters should
   drive a sex scene.
4. The relationship your characters have to each other—
   whether they are adulterers or strangers on a train—is critical to what happens in a sex scene.

I explain and illustrate many of these ideas in two chapters of
basic principles that could be mapped onto almost every kind of
sexual encounter or relationship you are moved to write about. In
other chapters I delve into six types of sexual relationships (first

times, honeymoons, married people, casual lovers, etc.) and use examples from contemporary fiction that illustrate particular principles, so that you can apply them to your own work.

I use as many examples as I can to suggest the variety of possibilities, but also to urge you to read more deeply and closely, for two vital reasons: so you can ultimately read your own work as critically as you read someone else's, and so you can study *any* sex scene from here on out and absorb its lessons as you need them.

I chose the examples I did for literary and nonliterary reasons: quality, length, clarity, and their ability to make sense in excerpted form with a minimum of explanation. I could not use dozens of truly wonderful passages because they were too long or did not deliver all their goods out of context. I do not mean that the selections I have made should stand as the only approved ways to write about sex in fiction, or as the only styles in which to write about sex. Like a sex manual, this book is meant to float ideas you may not have considered and give you permission to indulge them. Unlike a set of instructions for building a submarine, these ideas do not have to be strictly adhered to, inch for inch, in order to be of use.

I have purposely limited my examples to those from recently written fiction, not to dismiss the work of writers from Boccaccio to D. H. Lawrence, but because writing about sex is influenced so strongly by the attitudes of the culture in which it is written. The older examples, as I read them, do not suggest all the possibilities—in terms of directness, attitudes, and idioms—that are available to writers today. I hope that, when armed with new powers to read and analyze a scene, the writer who is writing historical fiction can turn to older examples, where they exist, and learn what he or she needs to know about the language and sensibilities of the period. Two examples I did use from recent work—*Plains Song* and *Chang and Eng*—are set in the nineteenth century.

The Joy of Writing Sex is not an encyclopedia of sexual tastes and habits. The variety of human sexual experience is too vast to be included in a book meant to help writers sharpen their prose and their literary faculties. You will notice, sooner or later, that I do not offer a single hint on writing about sex with animals. I am not saying it is unthinkable, unimaginable, or beyond the realm of literature (see Stanley Elkin's novella *The Making of Ashburham*, in which a man makes love to and falls in love with a bear; Ted Mooney's novel *Easy Travel to Other Planets*, ditto a woman and a dolphin; and a satiric send-up of the subject in Francine Prose's *Blue Angel*), but my focus in this book is on the nature of the relationship between sex partners, and it is beyond my own limited imagination and experience to offer any generally applicable insights as to how a cow would respond to even the most ardent advances.

Readers will also not find guidance for writing about rape and other forms of sex-related violence. I had originally intended to include such a chapter, but when I sat down to write it, I realized the subject was violence, not sex, and the relationship between partners was between a criminal and his or her victim. There is a great deal to say on this subject, but I was soon convinced that this is not the place to say it.

Though *The Joy of Writing Sex* is also not intended to free you to give voice to your sexual fantasies, desires, traumas, or troubles, do not let the principles and exhortations about good writing inhibit you from delving into your personal material in whatever way feels necessary, whether or not the writing ever becomes fiction. In my interview with her, novelist and short story writer Dorothy Allison emphasized the importance of this freedom to write:

> If I hadn't learned to write about sex, and particularly to write about my own sexual desires, I don't think I would have survived. I think the guilt, the terror I grew up with was so extraordinarily powerful that if I had not written my way out of it, I'd be dead. . . . And I think it's vital [to write about],

aside from whether it ever becomes good fiction, particularly for women with transgressive sexuality . . . [or] people who in any way feel that their own sexuality cannot be expressed. Writing can be a way to find a way to be real and sane in the world, even if it feels a little crazy while you're doing it.

In almost every discussion I've had about *The Joy of Writing Sex*, I'm asked: Who does it best? For several decades, my personal favorite has been James Salter, who writes with extraordinary elegance and compression about sex and everything else. I said in the first edition of *Joy* that I would take a page of Salter's from *A Sport and a Pastime* over a shelf of Anaïs Nin. I sent him a copy of the book when it was published; he wrote to me and admitted that now that so many others write about sex in their fiction, he no longer does.

I've recently read Edmund White's trilogy—*A Boy's Own Story, The Beautiful Room Is Empty,* and *The Farewell Symphony*—and would add him to my list of favorites. His work—and his own history—could not be more different from Salter's. As a teenager in the Midwest in the 1950s, he was sent to a boy's boarding school and to a psychoanalyst, both to be "cured" of his homosexuality. As our preeminent gay literary writer—though the term ought not deter readers of all persuasions from his splendid work—he has chronicled the trajectory of gay life in the second half of the twentieth century, an extraordinary time of sexual repression, liberation, and tragedy. He wrote in *The Beautiful Room*, "The most important things in our intimate lives can't be discussed with strangers, except in books." Fortunately for us, we have his.

We also have the work of Philip Roth, who has devoted himself to examining the psyche and sex life of a certain generation of straight American male, with results that are often brilliant, often hilarious, and always worth reading, even when they abrade and annoy.

Recently, I found Susanna Moore's *In the Cut* to be erotic, thrilling, bold, and disturbing—with an intensity few writers manage to sustain.

But the broader answer to the question of my favorites is that I have been on the lookout here, not for the Best Sexy Writer Around, but for encounters and descriptions that engage us aesthetically and emotionally, that bring us deeper into the story, more palpably into the lives of the characters, that strike the right tone and appear at precisely the right moment. I am deeply impressed with the seduction scene in Elizabeth Strout's novel *Amy and Isabelle,* and regret it is too long to include here. A fatherless fifteen-year-old girl is befriended over a period of months by a Humbert Humbert–like high school teacher; their first physical contact beyond a kiss takes place in a car. They never get further than foreplay in this scene that is beautifully written, remarkably erotic, and remarkably creepy at the same time.

Rosellen Brown is not someone whose books are chocked with steamy sex, but the bedroom scene in her 1992 novel *Before and After* has stayed with me, not because the sex she describes makes the earth move or because the description of it is lapidary, but because the setting and dialogue leading up to and following it are so believable and wrenching, because they reveal so much to us about these characters at a time of crisis and, ultimately, so much to us about ourselves.

1

WHAT WILL MY GRANDMOTHER THINK?: TALKING TO WRITERS ABOUT SEX

There is no safety in writing well.
                              —DOROTHY ALLISON
                              (In an interview for this book)

I owe the idea for this chapter of interviews with writers to my late grandmother, for her unvarnished reaction to my first novel, *Slow Dancing*. She rarely telephoned me, so I was startled to hear her voice that night. "I just finished your book," she announced, "and I am *not* impressed. This book you're writing now, is *this* going to be a book your grandmother will like?"

It was not necessary for her to explain the problem, which began in the first sentence, with the character declaring that sleeping with men she did not care about was an acquired taste and that she had acquired it. It had what I thought was a happyish, girl-gets-nice-guy ending, given where it began, but my grandmother did not see it that way.

She was too frail to read the next novel and did not live to read the third. But her bald statements about the first led me to sense a need for a chapter about how we handle the internal and external censors in our writing lives, now that paid censors have been forced into new lines of work.

My thought was to put this question to writers who have written sex scenes of notable excellence. I wanted to be sure to talk to straight and gay writers, to writers of different generations, and—in something of a twist—to a few writers who have chosen *not* to write explicitly about sex while nevertheless delving into the nature and operation of romantic relationships. In deciding to contact Darin Strauss, author of *Chang and Eng,* a first novel based loosely on the real lives of the original Siamese twins who married a pair of sisters in North Carolina and fathered twenty-one children, I was more purely curious about why Strauss made the choices he made in creating his novel's sex scenes.

Reading over interviews with Edmund White, Dorothy Allison, Alan Hollinghurst, and Joseph Olshan, who have written explicitly about gay and lesbian sexual relationships and, in Allison's case, childhood incest, it's clear they come to write about sex and sexuality from a vastly different set of personal and cultural struggles than do heterosexual writers who came of age in the 1960s and early '70s. Compared to the straight writers in this small sample, these gay and lesbian writers talk much more about their lack of historic role models in writing about sex and about their sense of purpose, daring, and sometimes shame, in telling outsiders things we do not know about their culture, whether it's the community of incest survivors, gay men before AIDS, or gay men who long for sex, love, and commitment here and now.

Though I started out with grandmothers on my mind, the arsenal of questions quickly grew as writers gave unexpected answers to my sometimes too guarded inquiries. In a letter to John Updike, preeminent critic and author of some forty often very sexually explicit novels and short story and poetry collections, I quite primly asked, "Are there writers whose sex scenes you feel do as much for character development as your scenes do?"

He wrote back, "Writing my sex scenes physically excites me, as it should. I don't enjoy other writers' as much as my own, but Iris Murdoch in *The Sacred and Profane Love Machine* does bravely try to show sexual compatibility and passion in an otherwise incompatible couple." From then on I got a little nosier with the writers I interviewed and asked them whether their own work aroused them.

I do not have room to publish each interview and letter I received in its entirety. Instead, to paraphrase Bob Dylan, I have tried to synthesize and categorize, in an attempt to squeeze as many voices into this space as I could. Bits of the interviews also appear throughout the book, wherever they seem to help make a point. In the case of the late Jerome Badanes, I have made an exception and include here a long section of our interview, which took place four days before he died unexpectedly in 1995. His only novel, the extraordinary *Final Opus of Leon Solomon*, published to much acclaim in 1989 by Knopf, is no longer in print. I hope this interview encourages readers to seek out his novel, which won the Edward Lewis Wallant Award for Best Jewish Novel of the Year.

I conducted interviews by phone or in person with Dorothy Allison, Russell Banks, John Casey, Jane DeLynn, Janice Eidus, Deborah Eisenberg, Stephen McCauley, Joseph Olshan, and Edmund White. Alan Hollinghurst, Carol Shields, and John Updike were kind enough to reply in writing to my letters. Charles Baxter and Darin Strauss answered my questions via e-mail.

Q. *Who are your censors and how do you silence them?*
A. *Just do it.*

Canadian writer Robertson Davies was a dutiful son. He said publicly that he waited until his parents were dead to publish his "important fiction." His mother died in 1948, three years before he published his first novel; his father died in 1967, three years before *Fifth Business* appeared, the first of the novels in the celebrated *Deptford Trilogy*, which put Davies on the international literary map. In the spring of 1995, radio interviewer Terry Gross, the host of the nationally syndicated *Fresh Air*, asked him what he feared his parents would object to in his work. "It would have embarrassed them," he said simply. "I think because of my attitudes toward a great many things, including sex. I didn't want to distress them, so I didn't write about that kind of thing in the way I eventually did until after they were no longer here."

None of the writers I interviewed took such drastic measures, though novelist Jane DeLynn made a preemptive strike and silenced her censors at the source when she published her fourth novel, *Don Juan in the Village*, a bold, urgent account of a lonely lesbian's sexual adventures over the last few decades. Though DeLynn had written about sex in her fiction before, this novel had, in her words, "much more sex and much more variety."

Jane DeLynn: My father is now dead, though he was alive at the time the book came out. I very easily got him to promise not to read it because I had published an essay having nothing to do with sex, about the Holocaust. It was a personal essay and it had touched on my parents, and he was really angry about that, much more so than my mother. He was very happy to agree not to read the novel if I suggested it might disturb him. My mother was harder to persuade, but I eventually made her promise. She wouldn't promise not to read it, but I said, "If you read it, we're just not going to talk about it. You have to promise you're not going to get mad at me if you read it, because you're forewarned." And she did agree. . . .

I don't really find writing about sex necessarily more intimate than writing about other subjects. [In writing *Don Juan*] I had a kind of distanced attitude toward even experiences that might be similar to what I've gone through. I really think that writing about sex is writing about the mind. Once the book was sold, I began to worry about my parents, but I can't say that was much of a consideration. And lovers I didn't worry about at all.

Celebrated short story writer and novelist Charles Baxter, whose most recent novel, *The Feast of Love*, has brought him a wide readership, has not felt the pressures of internal or external censorship. To the contrary.

Charles Baxter: I was actually afraid that my writing on this subject might be dull or banal, rather than "shocking." Thornton Wilder in his journals says that an adult is rarely shocked—that being shocked is usually a pose. I believe that. People pretend to be shocked to get an advantage on you. Eighty percent of shock is faked. When my friends have been surprised by some of these sections I've written, it is only because—they claim—they were surprised that I had some knowledge of some subject they didn't think I knew about. They preferred to think I was ignorant, or innocent.

Edmund White, author of many novels, biographies of Jean Genet and Marcel Proust, and coauthor of *The Joy of Gay Sex*, is the most esteemed gay writer in America today. At the age of fifteen, he wrote what he calls "a gay novel," with no models whatsoever for the genre; nor at the time had he read any pornography, gay or otherwise. When he began writing fiction as an adult, he did not feel constrained by inhibition.

Edmund White: I think I'm an exhibitionist in terms of writing. [Early on] maybe there was even a secret sexual thrill in writing so openly about myself. I was much more assertive in my writing than I was in my life. More assertive, and franker, about sex, but more assertive about gay identity than I was in life.

My mother was a psychologist and was very open about talking about sex, including her own sex life. I guess since I was psychoanalyzed at a very early age, I was also disinhibited about talking about sex, which was obviously one of the main subjects in psychoanalysis, which I started at age fifteen. I continued off and on for the next twenty years, so this is very much part of my kind of overobserved life.

I've been interviewed about my life and the interviewer will assume that because I write so explicitly about sex I'm willing to talk about it and that there's no distinction between the work and my life. But when I started with *A Boy's Own Story,* which came out in 1982, the convention still reigned that if you called it a novel, it was a novel, and so an interviewer at that time would still tiptoe around and say, "In your novel, the protagonist, who might or might not be based on you . . ." We live in the era of memoir now and people don't have a shield. Now it's "Why did you do that?"

Though Dorothy Allison's short fiction and essays had been known for many years to those who follow lesbian writing, it was not until she published her first novel, *Bastard Out of Carolina,* in 1992, about a poor Southern girl brutalized by her stepfather's incest and beatings, that Allison reached a wider audience. In addition to the literary acclaim the novel brought her, she has found herself a role model for lesbians, incest survivors, and others with what she calls "transgressive sexuality . . . people who in any way feel that their own sexuality cannot be expressed." Over the years she has "been trying to encourage the creation of women's sexual literature," she told me, through her support of new magazines and teaching writing workshops.

Dorothy Allison: My family does not include people who read or . . . the only thing [they] read is popular magazines, self-help books and mysteries. . . . In their minds to write at all is so scary that I didn't have to be afraid of shocking them by writing anything sexually explicit or revealing the fact that I'm a lesbian or even talking about incest. . . . So my family was not the fear. . . . [My fear] was the good girls. . . . I was scared of that middle-class female to whom I have been on occasion sexually attracted and who always seemed like a strange and exotic creature to me, and I was afraid she would think I was [a] demented, evil creature. . . . The other category of good girl was good feminist. Feminism gave me an enormous amount of authority to write about sex and class and my own life at the same time as it set up some really rigid barriers about *how* I could write about it. It was very difficult to write the sections of *Bastard* in which [the narrator] Bone is clearly having profoundly masochistic sexual fantasies. Most of my feminist ideology told me either I was not to talk about that or I was supposed to construct it so that you saw immediately that this was not the child's desire, it was the thing handed to her. It was entirely induced by the sexual assaults by her stepfather and that it didn't have any connection to anything else, which isn't true—the victim ideology that says this isn't something that comes out of you, or that it's anything to deal with . . .

Keep in mind that *Bastard* was published when I was forty-three. I had been writing for twenty years before I managed to finish that novel. It took a long time to stop those voices and write past them.

I don't think the voices have quieted down. I can keep them under control sometimes! Essentially I think that the last decade gave me some tools. One was other women writers who were trying to do some of the same kind of things I wanted to do. Basically I wanted to write about sexuality and the construction of sexual desire in a very complicated forthright manner, and there were some other writers who were doing that. I think my friendship with writers Joan Nestle and Pat Califia helped a lot. They are two polar opposites. Both are trying to examine sexual desire as an outlaw. Joan is one of the people who organizes the Lesbian Herstory Archives in New York. [Pat Califia is the author of *Macho*

Sluts and *Sapphistry.*] In my mind, Joan was more respectable than I was. Pat was more of an outlaw. I could be in this dancing place kind of in the middle.

Reviewers praised Darin Strauss's first novel, *Chang and Eng,* published in 2000, for his bold choice of subject—history's eponymous Siamese twins, born in Siam, in 1811—and the powers of invention, imagination, and empathy he hung on a slender historical record. It's known that Chang and Eng Bunker married sisters in North Carolina and fathered twenty-one children. Regarding their sexual relations, they "developed a method by which the inactive brother tried to give the busier one a little privacy," Strauss wrote me. "Beyond that, I invented."

I asked Strauss why he made the choices he had about the tenor and details of the sex scenes, and whether he felt self-conscious or to any degree "censored" as he wrote them.

Darin Strauss: I knew I had to include at least one sex scene in the novel—because, of course, here's the main thing people want to know: "How did they do it?" My choices largely involved deciding how *much* actually to portray. I didn't want to write anything that would have been unseemly. Because I think the danger with a story like the one I chose to tell is that, in inept hands, it might easily veer toward the crass and sensationalistic. I wasn't interested in cheap voyeurism with these sex scenes, in making the book a literary variant of the freak shows that took such awful advantage of Chang and Eng while they lived. What I *did* want to do is to make the reader aware of how odd, surprising, comic, thrilling, and exceptionally romantic the first experience of physical love would have felt to men born as they had been—and I wanted to do that without being exploitative or boorish.

But I don't think I approached my sex scenes in a different way than I would have when writing about any other, more "normal" intimacy. A well-rendered sexual moment always, I think, has to be about what's going on with the characters' lives—and all the particulars of context that go with that—as much as it should be about the actual process of screwing. In that way, a sex scene is like any other. If you write about two characters going out for ice cream, you shouldn't ignore all the important dramatic and thematic stuff you've gone to such pains to build, in order merely to describe how sensational mint chocolate chip tastes as it goes into their mouths.

I knew that there were specific challenges with telling this story, questions of staying within the bounds of good taste, that might have made my conjoined characters' sex scenes difficult for me. Yet I don't think I ever got hung up about shushing any internal censors. But my girlfriend was very anxious to read those scenes. She said that she was scared I'd relay personal details about our sex lives onto the page, and so she was nervous about her parents reading it. But since neither of us has been joined to a sibling during the sex act, she shouldn't have worried.

If Strauss's girlfriend discovered she had nothing to worry about once the book was published, Strauss learned that the sex scenes had gotten the attention of people he had not thought to consider.

Darin Strauss: I attended the Bunker family reunion in North Carolina a month after the hardcover came out. At this point Chang and Eng have about 1,800 descendants, and a good number of them attend these bi-yearly reunions. A few of the descendants said, "I'm a little annoyed that you took the story of our great-grandparents and wrote about them fucking." And I understood where they were coming from. A book is just a book, but a family history is sacred. But, you know, when I was writing this story, I didn't know if I'd even sell it; the last thing I thought was that these characters I scribbled about in my underwear before sunup would have flesh-and-blood progeny who'd get pissed off by my work. So, when I met these people, I had to explain the differences between fiction and biography to some of them, and also that, if I was going in any way to do this story justice, in all its aspects, then to have avoided writing sex scenes would have been a cop-out.

Most non-Bunker people I've talked to about my book have really liked the sex scenes, though. They're often a big hit at the readings.

Joseph Olshan, author of many novels, including *Clara's Heart*, and most recently *Vanitas* and *Nightswimmer*, an erotically charged journey through gay New York in the 1990s, admits that he had to "trick" himself into writing explicitly in *Nightswimmer*. "When you were writing the sex scenes in *Nightswimmer*," I asked him, "was it straightforward or did you have to dig deep?"

Joseph Olshan: I had to dig deep. I had to kind of trick myself. I had this feeling that the richest material one has as a writer is the part that one has to trick oneself into writing, because in a way it's what the psyche guards against. Your best stories, your best material, your most lyrical lines are the ones hardest to get to because there's something in you that doesn't want that to come out, that doesn't want that to be exposed. You know when the body goes into shock when you get hurt, it's the same kind of thing. You've got to really wake yourself up in a way, to get to that part. If I thought about all the people who were going to read the scenes when I sat down to write them, I probably wouldn't do it. . . .

[Yet] I think I am one person who should probably be writing about sex. It seems to come naturally to me. It's something I think a lot about. Not the act of sex but the dynamics of the relationship and what it means. And love and loneliness and obsession. . . . When I think about the sex scenes in *Nightswimmer* . . . reaching orgasm is not the important thing. . . . Very few of the sex scenes actually reach orgasm. It's the connection, it's how people finally connect when they get into the rhythm of making love. Once that happens it's not as interesting. . . . But it's fascinating for the outside world to see how the two heavenly bodies dock, become synchronized.

Writers are not the only ones in this relationship between writer and reader who rely on tricks to help them through the difficult passages. Russell Banks, author of some fifteen works of fiction, including the novels *Cloudsplitter, Continental Drift, Affliction, The Sweet Hereafter,* and *Rule of the Bone,* told me that he has never censored himself when writing about sexual matters, partly, he thinks, because of a freedom his mother gave him years ago, when his second novel was published.

Russell Banks: My mother is a born-again Christian. I love her and admire her and am very close to her. She's fastidious about language. My second novel has some pretty bizarre sex scenes. They're comic in a way. They're very broad and reckless. It's not realistic fiction at all. My mother told me she had read the book. I said, "But what about all those dirty parts, Mom?" She said, "As soon as I hear them coming, I jump ahead." I talked to her recently about them and she says she still does it that way.

British novelist Alan Hollinghurst, whose first novel, *The Swimming-Pool Library,* has the stature of a contemporary gay classic, characterizes his descriptions of gay sex in that novel as "unapologetic." His answer, in writing, to my questions about internal and external censors was refreshingly uncomplicated.

Alan Hollinghurst: I did not have to overcome any reluctance to write sex scenes. I was apprehensive about how my parents would react to the book, but after initial disconcertment they became interested in it, and in its success.

Whether we already possess or still need to cultivate Hollinghurst's un-self-conscious approach to the subject, it is useful to keep John Casey's advice—suitable for framing—in mind. Casey is the author of the novels *The Half-Life of Happiness, Spartina,* which won the National Book Award, and *An American Romance,* which a friend of mine described as "Henry James with sex."

John Casey: There is a potency [in writing explicitly about sex] you have to be careful of, because it can disrupt the reader's experience of reading the book. But you *can't* think about the reader—any reader—over your shoulder when you're writing. You can go back later and you can worry about people's qualms. When you're alone in your working room, you can't think about anyone.

Q. *What's love got to do with it?*
A. *Maybe nothing.*

When the most elementary facts of life were first explained to me, in about 1962, it was still commonly held in middle-class families where children were being raised that only married people had sex and had babies, and that love should be a requirement for both. When I was a bit older, my mother told me that the only people who went to bed with those they weren't in love with were men; a woman should want nothing more than to save herself for her husband. She knew I would grow up to be such a woman.

The world changed. My mother changed. Love quit being a requirement for sexual intimacy. Or maybe what happened is that women came to have the option of sex without love that men had always had. In any case, in literature now, as in life and on television, choosing to go to bed with someone you aren't married to and aren't in love with can be as unremarkable a decision as buying a tank of gas. The word *seduction* has gone out of fashion. Who needs to be seduced when it's okay for us to be so willing?

One of my favorite casual sex scenes in recent fiction occurs in Carolyn See's 1999 comic novel, *The Handyman*, when Bob, a hapless twenty-eight-year-old aspiring artist who has just moved into a group house for the summer in Los Angeles, comes upon his female housemate watching a TV cooking show in the middle of the day.

> "So, Kate? Want to do it?"
> *"No!"*
> "Why not?"
> "Are you crazy?". . .
> She gave a last look at the television, where some guy was getting busy with a whisk, and crunched herself up off the bed.
> "Your room," she said, "but keep it quiet."

A page later, when it's over, Bob asks the clichéd question, "How was it for you?" but her answer is hardly predictable: "Well," she said kindly, "have you ever had a TV dinner?"

Love and sex have been so separate for the last few decades that critic Vivian Gornick recently published *The End of the Novel of Love*, based on her essay of the same name. She argued that romantic love is no longer "an organizing principle" in fiction; that it no longer has the power to "achieve a sense of the tragic or the inevitable," as it did earlier in the twentieth century, and certainly in the great nineteenth-century novels about adultery. Today, when love fails us, we routinely divorce, go into therapy, and find another spouse, whom we will find deficient sooner or later. My own sense is that the novel of love has been superseded by the novel that explores the primacy of our sexual selves. When I posed this idea to Charles Baxter—whose *The Feast of Love* is a rich symphony of interlocking stories about romantic love, parental love, and sexual connection—he agreed.

Charles Baxter: I often thought of Vivian Gornick's book while I was writing my own. I was writing *The Feast of Love* partly as an answer to *The End of the Novel of Love* and once had an epigraph from that book at the beginning of my own until my editor removed it. Gornick's argument is that bourgeois life is over, and that the terrible sufferings associated with separations, divorces, and so on are pretty much a thing of the past. The subject has consequently lost its depth and weight. We do not judge our lives by whom we love or how successfully we love anymore. I'm not so sure, though she makes a very good case for her argument using one of Jane Smiley's stories ["The Age of Grief"]. Readers reacting to my book have been more surprised, I think, by the explicitness of the love than they have been by the explicitness of the sex (which is quite minor by contemporary standards).

I've only encountered one person who was taken aback by the events and language of the book, a sixty-five-year-old woman who told me that if she had been my mother, she would have washed out my mouth with soap; but a number of twenty-something reviewers have noted that the subject matter of the book—love— is rather retro. So maybe Vivian Gornick is correct.

Q. *What's hot and what's not?*
A. *You would be surprised.*

When I first began asking writers what books they found arousing or had when they were young, it was to educate myself. I assumed I would end up with a reading list of the smartest sexy books around—everything, I guessed, from Gustave Flaubert's *Madame Bovary* to Terry Southern's comic *Candy*. But most of the answers I got early in the process were so unexpected, I gave up all hope of amassing an erotic reading list and kept asking the question anyway—because the answers said so much about the quirky and uncategorizable nature of human sexuality. My sense I was on to something interesting began with John Casey telling me that two of the most memorable sexy novels of his youth were Stendhal's *The Charterhouse of Parma* and *The Red and the Black*. When he reread *The Charterhouse of Parma* years later, he was astonished to see there was much less passion in the scenes between Fabrizio and his aunt than he had remembered as an adolescent. "As a teenager with raging hormones you keep adding stuff to what's really there," he explains. In writing his own much more explicit sex scenes, what is important to him are not the mechanics but "the swoon. The delicious palpitations of one's heart is the real eroticism."

When I reported some of the early book titles to Jane DeLynn, she observed that what makes a memorable sexy book for many of us is "obviously in the realm of the mind." She confessed that for her "the sexiest scene in literature" occurs in Virginia Woolf's *Mrs. Dalloway*, in which the middle-aged Clarissa Dalloway, whose husband, a member of Parliament, had recently insisted she sleep alone in their attic, in a narrow bed, to help recover from an illness. As she fixes up the ascetic room and prepares for a big party she is giving that night, she thinks about "this question of love . . . this falling in love with women," and of her bold, sexually aware childhood friend Sally Seton, who kissed her once on the lips when they were nineteen. They had been walking on the terrace with other visitors to the house. "Then came the most exquisite moment of her whole life passing a stone urn with flowers in it. Sally stopped; picked a flower; kissed her on the lips. The whole world might have turned upside down!"

John Updike gave a reading list closer to the one I expected from other writers, which segues nicely into his thematic summaries of his own work.

John Updike: Joyce and Lawrence, of course, as models of novelists who took sex in stride in their representations of life; but also Edmund Wilson's *Hecate County* and the novels of Erskine Caldwell and James M. Cain, who within the bounds of '30s–'40s possibility wrote about sex in a way that made a strong impression on an adolescent boy. And Norman Mailer's groundbreaking story of 1958, "The Time of Her Time," which I read with astonishment while standing in a bookstore. After 1961 and Henry Miller and Grove Press, the frontier challenge was replaced by a need to farm the opened-up territory with real and interesting accounts of sex lives as part of lives. *Couples,* for instance, was about an illicit couple bonding through fellatio. *A Month of Sundays* tried to show impotence as an effect of moral scruple. In *Rabbit Is Rich,* married love is played for a certain comedy, and [in] the scene with Thelma and Rabbit buggery and water games are presented rather tenderly, as attempts, in a sex-saturated world, to make an impression and live up to the surrounding porn culture. Pornography and theology in *Roger's Version* are seen as kindred mental exercises, both delicious.

For Carol Shields, an American-born Canadian writer whose fifth novel, *The Stone Diaries,* won the Pulitzer Prize in 1995, a scene in a short story by Alice Munro, "Bardon Bus," is her favorite erotic encounter in print. Shields is a wickedly astute chronicler of the quirks and longings of ordinary people who turn out to be not so ordinary, a sort of Jane Austen with sex. In a letter to me, she described a moment from her own life:

> The most erotic scene I've ever witnessed was my uncle bending over at the dining room table to kiss the back of my aunt's neck. It was summertime and she was wearing a sundress and just lifting a spoonful of sherbet to her lips. They were middle-aged then. I was a child, maybe nine or ten. But I rec-

ognized "it.". . . . I thought I might try to write about this experience. But all the old problems occur—how to make such a small gesture *felt*.

The work of novelist and award-winning short story writer Janice Eidus is often set in New York City and steeped in classic myths retold in contemporary urban life. For example, "Ladies with Long Hair" was inspired by the death from AIDS of Eidus's hairdresser. In the *Lysistrata*-based story, women whose hairdressers have all died of AIDS become politicized; they refuse to cut their hair again until a cure is found, and with their long, long locks, they stage protests and demonstrations.

Janice Eidus: When I was about twelve I read *Romeo and Juliet* and I thought it was *just* the most erotic thing on earth, and when I started thinking about other books that have mattered to me in terms of erotic arousal or passion, I realize that there are certain kinds of scenes that *Romeo and Juliet* has that are always in these other books . . . an obsessive desire that's unleashed in both the women and the men, not an unrequited passion. *Adele H.* [the movie that tells the story of Victor Hugo's daughter's obsessive fixation on a one-time lover] is not quite as erotic to me as when both are really touched in this way, when there's a defiance of convention—the forbidden that's good and ethical, because I'm really such a humanist. One of the things I find unerotic in fiction, and a lot of contemporary fiction has it, is nihilism, people who defy convention but in a very bloodless, cold-blooded way. . . . Do you know Angela Carter's writing? I love all her novels. A few I read when I discovered her ten years ago I thought were incredibly erotic. They use a kind of mythology and sexuality combined. There's something almost beautiful about using these age-old myths and reinventing them in a contemporary sexualized context. . . . You know the archetypes and they very often follow the kind of defiance of convention and tremendous risk in the name of a very positive desire in love.

In a slightly different form, I put the sexy-book question to Alan Hollinghurst. Had there been particular books and authors he felt had given him permission to write about his characters' sex lives?

Alan Hollinghurst: I suppose like anyone, but particularly perhaps like any gay person with literary inclinations, I tried to find accounts of gay sexual experiences in books, but of course in the best authors the sex scenes were often deeply colored by some other preoccupation—e.g., in Genet or Burroughs. I always found those "scandalous" sex books of the '50s and '60s, posing as exposés or as a kind of social anthropology or as somehow "medical," to be terribly depressing. I had done work as a graduate student on earlier gay writers (specifically Forster, Firbank, and L. P. Hartley) who hadn't been able to write openly about their sexuality, but had created fascinating opportunities for expressing it in oblique or coded forms. And then there were the (generally very routine and fantastic) stories in porno magazines. It's hard to think back to intentions of ten years ago or more [when he was writing *The Swimming-Pool Library*]; but I do remember feeling that the segregation of experience into the Forsterian cryptic and the baldly pornographic did some deep violence to the way life was actually lived and felt, where sexual thoughts and deeds (especially in the case of a beautiful and promiscuous young gay man, as in *The Swimming-Pool Library*) were intimately wrapped up with everything else in life. Hardly anyone writing literary novels about gay life, it seemed to me, had really been prepared to mix the sex in in this essentially realistic way; there was a bit in [Edmund White's] *A Boy's Own Story*, but *The Beautiful Room Is Empty*, which has far more sex in it, had not yet come out. I agree with Edmund White that it felt like quite a novel thing to be doing at that time. So no, I don't think there were other authors who gave me permission to write about my characters' sex lives in the way I did.

Q. *Does your own work turn you on?*
A. *Not always.*

Dorothy Allison: No, not by the time it's finished! In the early stages, yes, sometimes, but not by the time I've worked it down and gotten it in publishable form.

Charles Baxter: Very rarely for me, my own. Almost never. One builds one's funhouse for others, not for oneself. Usually they're so hard to write well that I can't imagine finding them arousing myself, because I've spent so much time on them. I see every prop, every piece of dialogue, the way a stage director sees them: there they are, I put them there, every last one.

Alan Hollinghurst: No, I'm not physically excited by writing about sex; the point for me has always been to write about it with as steady an eye as I try to bring to bear on everything else. So much sex writing goes wrong. . . . Anyway, much of the sex I describe [in *The Swimming-Pool Library* and *The Folding Star*] is not great sex; it's fleeting, or absurd, or unhappy or unsatisfactory in some way.

For many writers and readers, the sexiest writing operates on the metonymy principle, which John Casey describes this way: "If you have one thing stand for another, it tends to heighten all the things that aren't being talked about." For many writers and readers, suggestion, suppression, and sublimation are more potent aphrodisiacs than the real thing. Carol Shields reported that she wrote an academic paper several years ago about

Jane Austen's use (non-use, really) of body parts in her books. (Fortunately, there is a concordance available.) There are something like two ankles and one nose in all those books. Also three breasts, but all belonging to men. And so the rise on the erotic thermometer is signaled obliquely, a flutter of a hand standing in for a major sexual response—all of it on this curious miniaturized scale, like looking into the doll house of sensuality.

Q. *What's the best advice about writing sex you've gotten?*
A. *Harold Brodkey's.*

Edmund White: I think one of the most influential things anybody ever said to me was something Harold Brodkey said. I was very friendly with him in the mid-1970s. He said to me, "Anybody who ever wrote 'She went down on him' is lying." I said, "What do you mean?" He said, "That assumes you know what 'going down on' is, that it's always the same no matter who does it, or that no matter which time an individual is doing it, even to the same partner." He said, "The truth is every time you make love it's entirely different, it's as though you've never done it before and no one else has done it, and if you as a writer can't capture that, you've failed."

I think that's really brilliant and absolutely true. Of course, he's that kind of phenomenologist about everything, and it's part of his downfall finally, in his last destroyed masterpiece, that he couldn't stop reinventing every fucking moment. You almost have to agree to have flat moments as well as round moments. If you round every moment and reinvent everything, it gets slowed down to a glacial pace and there's no relief and it's excruciating.

Q. *Is sex the most revealing thing you can write about?*
A. *Not anymore.*

Charles Baxter: Sexual explicitness is not the most revealing gesture we can make. Things have been turned upside down. In an age of exhibitionism, of the *Jerry Springer Show*, it's almost easier for a person to show his/her genitals than it is to show, or to reveal, love, or for that matter vulnerability. We have worked very hard to achieve sexual openness, and it's a wonderful thing, but tenderness and forbearance shouldn't be lost in the process. Contemporary cultural irony tolerates casual sexual relations better than professions of love or vulnerability. Who is more naked, the person who takes all clothes off, or the person who says, "I love you"?

Edmund White: Richard Sennett, the head of the New York Institute for the Humanities and critic, once said to me, "Edmund you'll tell anyone about your sex life, but you'll never confide in anyone your ideas." I think that's true. The so-called confessional statements that are supposedly about your most intimate things like your sex life—I'm much more open about things like that, and I've even worked it into party routines, than I am about my ideas, such as they are.

Q. *Is sex necessary?*
A. *Not always.*

Deborah Eisenberg, whose short stories have been published over the last twenty years in *The New Yorker*, have won many awards, and are gathered in three collections, *All Around Atlantis*, *Transactions in a Foreign Currency*, and *Under the 82nd Airborne*, decided that the explicit sex route was not for her. Her insights about the limitations of writing explicitly about sex also serve as advice to those who take sex on: Be specific.

Deborah Eisenberg: I don't really feel that there are special problems involved in writing about sex—I mean, in writing directly and graphically about sex—but I think maybe the same problems that are involved in writing about anything are likely to be exaggerated. The anatomical possibilities are limited, so a poorly written sex scene can be a little like hearing an eight-year-old describe the plot of his favorite movie. And on the other hand, because every reader brings to every sex scene *vivid* prior experience, writing graphically about sex can also be a little like writing: *dead mother.* You'll get a response, all right, but it might not be the response you want, or the response that proceeds from all the careful work you've done to show exactly what's happening between these two particular people—or these twelve particular people—right now. The hazard is that if you, the writer, are insufficiently in control, the response you'll get is the one that the reader would have had to any sex scene whatsoever that came his or her way. The problems of cliché and generality, which are exactly what writing is a battle against, are especially hard to outwit when you're writing about sex because the reader's response is so likely to be automatic and blinding. It's as if a flash were going off, obscuring all the specifics and detail and nuance you've constructed so carefully about your characters and their encounter. Of course, that's the way sex sometimes works in real life—you know: Well, I actually don't happen to care just now *who* that person is—and if that's what you want, fine.

I haven't really written that often, I suppose, directly about sex. Who knows what I'll feel like doing in the future, but up till now, it seems I've been somewhat more interested in the thwarted impulse, or something of the sort—the erotic charge inappropriately pervading all sorts of experience. And to me—well, there's all of *Madame Bovary,* of course, but one of the most sexually interesting *scenes* in literature is in *Anna Karenina* when Vronsky returns to his barracks after seeing Anna, and his roommate tells him an absolutely idiotic, very funny anecdote about helmets. Anna isn't in the scene at all—she's far away—but you're very aware of her. And the uncanny giddiness you experience along with Vronsky has to do, I think, with the shift in sexual power between Anna and him at that moment; the erotic obsession is like an animal that's released Vronsky temporarily, to settle its entire weight on Anna. The sexuality that's collapsed into that scene with the roommate is just so complex—and intense, and accurate, and *specific*.

When I originally interviewed Stephen McCauley in 1995, he talked about his reasons for not going into sexual detail in his three novels, *The Man of the House, The Easy Way Out*, and *The Object of My Affection*, comedies of manners that focus on gay relationships. He also spoke about the power of metonymy in *Lolita* and *Madame Bovary*.

In 2001, when I heard him read from his fourth novel, *True Enough*, I was surprised when two sets of characters fell, fairly explicitly, into bed together. McCauley was kind enough to share his thoughts about deciding to take the plunge in *True Enough*, a scene from which I discuss in chapter 7. His new comments follow those from the original interview:

Stephen McCauley (1995): *Madame Bovary,* for example, is filled with lush, sensual descriptions that heighten the reader's awareness of the erotic tension between the characters. The way Flaubert describes the texture of soot on a fireplace or the sound of water falling on a silk parasol or the look of Emma's tongue licking the bottom of a glass of liqueur conveys a powerful sense of sublimated sexuality. Flaubert's attention to all the senses is so exact and exquisite, he can write a powerful erotic scene with no physical contact. I suppose it helps to be a genius.

Sex scenes invariably fall flat when the urge to titillate or, worse still, to be titillated, overpowers a writer's attention to his or her characters. Like all scenes in fiction, a sex scene should be specific and deepen the reader's understanding of the characters. You can't do that if you lapse into an all-purpose, porn-inspired vocabulary for describing sex. When my first novel, *The Object of My Affection*, was published, it received some criticism in the gay press because it contained no explicit sex scenes. The attitude seemed to be that the book was unliberated or politically regressive because of that. But the narrator is extremely diffident. It would have been out of character for him to describe his sex life in detail—except for a few broad complaints—though there was no doubt in my mind that he was comfortable with his homosexuality. I convinced myself that there was something subversive in opting for no explicit sex. Of course, I'm open to the possibility that I'm just shy and repressed.

As a writer, you always want to lure your readers into the world of the book and keep them deeply immersed. With a certain kind of generically titillating sex scene, you run the risk of losing them completely, of sending them off into their own masturbatory fantasies rather than paying attention to what's going on in the novel.

Stephen McCauley (2001): It's certainly not the case that I felt one shouldn't write sex scenes, simply that it seemed somewhat wrong for the diffident first-person narrators I was writing about in my first three novels. In the case of *True Enough*, I realized that a lot of the problems in the marriage of one character, Jane, could be made concrete by showing her frustration and disappointment while having sex with her husband. And to do that effectively, I had to write an explicit, though hardly erotic scene. It emerged naturally in the writing. The fun for me was in finding the physical details that I hoped would make the reader cringe and laugh at the same time. I wanted readers to find Jane's dilemma funny and perhaps uncomfortably familiar. All of the details that ought to be erotic and titillating—the kisses, the tongue, the sweat, the shared heat, the engorged penis, the sensitized skin—are irritating and unnerving to the character. And so I was able (in my mind, anyway) to use some of the lovemaking clichés in an unexpected way. She's annoyed by the impressive size of her husband's penis; she's enraged by his solicitous tenderness.

I've always felt that a happy sex life kills a person's sense of humor about himself remarkably quickly. So writing the scenes of Jane's passionate lovemaking with her ex-husband was more of a challenge. Fortunately, she was so swamped with guilt about the affair, that it wasn't all bliss, no matter how erotically satisfying.

OVER THE TOP: EXCERPTS FROM AN INTERVIEW WITH JEROME BADANES

The narrator of Jerome Badanes's masterful novel, *The Final Opus of Leon Solomon,* an Auschwitz survivor and scholar of Jewish history, is about to commit suicide after being caught stealing papers from the New York Public Library. As he prepares to die, he writes his final opus on a stack of yellow legal pads, the story of his life. The novel includes many graphic sex scenes between people normally forbidden from intimate contact: Solomon and his sister, two Jews trying to pass for Aryans in Occupied Warsaw; and, four decades later in New York City, Solomon and the daughter of a Gestapo officer.

EB: The sex scenes in *The Final Opus of Leon Solomon* go against the advice we generally give people in writing about sex, that less is more. What made you take it so far over the top?

JB: First of all I don't write about sex at all. I mean, I have sex in my book, but I'm not sitting down to write sex. I'm sitting down to write something else. The sex is a vehicle to get to that other place. What I'm always trying to get to in my books is the ability of human beings to connect regardless of circumstances. So when I have my survivor have an affair with the daughter of a Nazi, they were trying to get past that history and they failed to. I made it as graphic as I did because I wanted the reader to experience with them both the desperation and the wondrousness of their attempt to get past it. I wanted the reader to be there through every detail, and I consider all those sexual details sacred. They're not smutty, they're not dirty, they're what people do. I wanted the reader to experience that, to feel them feeling the thrill of connection and the despair of knowing that the connection will be broken, that it can't be a lasting connection.

In the scenes with my main character when he's a young man and his sister that are on the edge of being totally incestuous, except they don't have intercourse, I wanted to get the reader close to it because I saw those scenes, as I said in the book, as a Kaddish for their lost youth and for their fate as Jews in Europe in occupied Warsaw. The Warsaw ghetto was just a few blocks away. . . . And to have the reader experience that Kaddish you had to go through the details. It's fine for the writers who just want to suggest things, but I felt I wanted to take the reader right there and take them to a place that is maybe awkward for them or embarrasses them or makes them nervous, but take them and keep pushing at it until the reader comes to that other place, and they feel what they felt. I don't believe in minimalization.

EB: You mean because you're dealing with something as disturbing as incest, so the reader can say yes, in that situation I might have done that?

JB: In some sense the moral imperative was for them to connect, both of them doomed, the sister totally doomed, the brother knowing that because of her rheumatoid arthritis. I want them to experience the degradation of having to go through all the taboo feelings, so I decided that instead of suggesting, I would say in detail what they did. Not using anything but descriptive language. . . . A reviewer talked about the sex, said that in a world turned upside down, the moral moment might include something as taboo-laden as incest. It's a comment on the world turned upside down. A comment on history. All the sex in *The Final*

Opus is in dire settings, deathly settings, as a way of remembering and being a moment of life in a death world, a way of creating a moment of good faith in a world filled with bad faith. . . .

Though I understood that and I felt that as the larger ambition . . . I wanted to make sure that it was sexy, so that the reader could experience it, and one way to make sure it's sexy is—the first way—to make sure I find it sexy. I wanted to feel sexy as I was writing about sex in even the most dangerous or tragic or historically horrifying circumstances, and that can make you feel a little bad, because you're feeling sexy about something horrible, but of course I wanted the reader to feel that, too. That itself is a paradox. And that's how the characters feel. And that was my way of doing that, so I tried to write sex scenes in such a way that the reader found them sexy, both men readers and women readers, and I was only hoping women readers, because I'm not a woman, but I could imagine myself into womanness in the scenes.

That was my goal. That's not easy to do. So that's why I couldn't do less is more. I wanted to really soak the reader in the details of sex so they could feel everything, so they could feel the paradox of it, sex while everyone's dying around them or they're about to be killed or they're breaking taboos. I wanted them to feel all that stuff, and I needed a lot of detail to do that. So that's why it's over the top, except I don't think it's over the top. I think it has to be over the top to be in the right place.

The Iliad graphically describes the killing of people. Not only the killing but the humiliation that people feel when they're totally at the mercy of the person who's about to kill them, and they're begging for their lives and they get murdered anyway, the way Achilles kills Hector. You get it from moment to moment. We can be very graphic about violence, but to be graphic about sex is a more complicated thing, apparently. Society has more trouble taking it. Actually, being that graphic about violence made the violence transcendent, it made you think about it, made you suddenly feel. When we see films of people getting shot we don't get a chance to feel what it is to be a person in the few seconds before death, totally at the mercy of the other person, someone who has totally lost his or her own will, totally enslaved at that moment before death. Homer gives that to us in some way, that modern thing that's been dumped. What I tried to do with the sex in *The Final Opus* was what I see being done with violence in *The Iliad*—deliver the moment in some way.

2

A SEX SCENE IS NOT
A SEX MANUAL
AND OTHER BASIC PRINCIPLES

Sex is something I really don't understand too hot. You
never know *where* the hell you are. I keep making up these
sex rules for myself, and then I break them right away.

—J. D. SALINGER,
The Catcher in the Rye

In the best fiction writing about sex, even if it is a brief paragraph,
we come to the end knowing not just "what happened" but something about the characters, their sensibilities, circumstances, or
inner lives, about the narrator who is relating the events, the concerns of the author—or all of the above. A well-written sex scene
engages us on many levels: erotic, aesthetic, psychological,
metaphorical, even philosophical.

Yet when reading a novel or short story whose sex scenes hook
us on all these levels, we are most often so fully in its thrall that we
don't analyze and compartmentalize our reactions; we just keep
reading and enjoying. But as we set out to learn to write a good

scene, like an apprentice auto mechanic, we need to study what's under the hood and find out how to take the engine apart before we learn how to put it back together.

As you embark on this endeavor, take a lesson Holden Caulfield had a hard time learning in *The Catcher in the Rye*: Don't even *think* about rules. There are no secret formulas, no shortcuts, no clever tricks to writing a good sex scene. Sex and fiction are much too particular, too personal—too unorganizable— to reduce them to a simple list of dos and don'ts. I offer instead, as John Gardner does in his informal textbook, *The Art of Fiction: Notes on Craft for Young Writers*, what he calls "general principles" that are broad enough to accommodate most every sexual appetite and literary style.

But before we get to those, let's look at three primary reasons why it can be so difficult to write well about sex in fiction:

1. Forty years ago, explicit sex scenes in fiction were almost nonexistent. Today they are as plentiful as pennies and, many would argue, about as valuable. When everything has already been said ad nauseam, how can we hope to make an original contribution?

2. Sex seems simple, but it isn't. As Edmund White explained in our interview: "Sex is the most intense dialogue that could possibly go on between two people in which you're never sure what the other person is thinking. It's like this passionate conversation with someone who speaks a different language or someone who can't hear, because unless they actually have a soundtrack going and are actually telling you what they're thinking and what's going through their heads, you don't know, and even then, that's often-times a pornographic soundtrack, which isn't the real thoughts they're actually having, because they're thinking, 'Maybe this will turn her on, or this.' There's so much strategy that goes on in people's heads during sex. More, less, harder, softer, maybe I should be romantic at this moment, maybe I should relent for a little bit. So there's always endless debate over strategy, and that is never confided."

Or, as E. M. Forster wrote—long before we could speak so openly about sex and sexuality—in his classic treatise on writing fiction, *Aspects of the Novel*: "When human beings love they try to get something. They also try to give something, and this double aim makes love more complicated than food or sleep. It is selfish and altruistic at the same time, and no amount of specialization in one direction quite atrophies the other."

The mechanics *are* simple, but the politics and psychodynamics—its hidden messages and meanings—make it the most complex of human exchanges. And despite sex saturation in the culture and sex education on TV, everything we need to know about our personal sexuality we must learn in the privacy of our own lives.

What makes sex so powerful an urge is our desire to connect with another human being. But as soon as you involve that other person—the Other—the equation is no longer simple. You long for an unfamiliar heartbeat against your skin but what you often get is someone else's heartache, someone colder and more distant than the warm body you sought, or someone as fragile and needy as you are. (Never, Nelson Algren cautions us, "sleep with someone whose troubles are worse than your own.") The costs of sexual intimacy can be exorbitant.

3. Sex means something different to each of us, and its meanings can multiply and change from minute to minute, evolve over time, as people and their cultures change. Sex can be an expression of affection, love, fear, vulnerability, anger, power, rage, submission—or nearly all of these at once. Sex strips us of our defenses, leaving us vulnerable to feelings that are often repressed.

THE TOP TEN

Writing fiction about sex is no more or less difficult than writing good fiction about anything else: committing every new word to paper leaves us wondering if we are headed in the right direction, and how we will know if we are not. But sex as a subject presents its own thorny challenges. Let's begin with ten general principles to help guide you as you slip between the sheets.

1. A sex scene is not a sex manual.
2. A good sex scene does not have to be about good sex.
3. It's okay—*really!*—to be sexually aroused by your own writing.
4. Your fear is your best friend.
5. Sex is nice, but character is destiny.
6. Only your characters know for sure (what to call it).
7. Take your cues from your characters.
8. Your characters must want and want intensely.
9. A good sex scene is always about sex and something else.
10. Who your characters are to each other is key.

Let's look at each of these more closely.

1. A sex scene or description is not a sex manual.
Writing about sex in fiction is different from writing about harpooning a whale; it's safe to assume your readers have had a good bit of experience with the former and almost none with the latter. We don't need a thorough report on the hydraulics unless they are relevant to your character's state of mind and your story's larger concerns (see, for example, the discussion of *Portnoy's Complaint* in chapter 3). "We know about the physiology," Russell Banks reminds us. "What a writer needs to tell us in a sex scene are the things we don't know."

For instance, we learn a certain character has a passion for pacifiers in this brief passage from *Love in the Time of Cholera,* a rich novel about lifelong love and passion by Colombian-born Nobel Prize–winner Gabriel García Márquez, which, he has said, was inspired by his parents' relationship. In this description, García Márquez says nothing about bodies or body parts, but Sara's pacifier ritual conveys all we need to know about the passionate, playful, and un-self-conscious nature of her sexual relationship with Florentino. By keeping our eyes on pacifiers rather than on body parts, in memorable, original fashion, the author reveals information about the lovers (Sara's lack of inhibition; Florentino's pleasure in that) and the culture that sanctions such a relationship. The pacifiers also remind us of sexual passion's power to hurl us back to elemental urges of infancy:

> What Florentino Ariza liked best about her was that in order to reach the heights of glory, she had to suck on an infant's pacifier while they made love. Eventually they had a string of them, in every size, shape, and color they could find in the market, and Sara Noriega hung them on the headboard so she could reach them without looking in her moments of extreme urgency.

2. A good sex scene does not have to be about good sex.
The aim of pornography, whether it's a movie or a magazine, is to arouse the consumer. Or as novelist and critic Cathleen Schine described it in the *New York Review of Books*, "Every pornographic narrative huffs and puffs to the same inexorable conclusion; tab A being fitted breathlessly into slot B. . . . However ornate the preparation, the outcome is inevitable." Coitus interruptus, disappointing sex, lovers who are less than enthusiastic in their coupling, a lover who drops off to sleep before the moment of truth—all would leave purveyors of porn demanding their money back. But in writing a sex scene in a serious piece of fiction, we have the privilege of lavishing our attention on characters who seem to flunk their major subject more often than they pass it. In fiction a sexual connection that goes awry or has cataclysmic consequences is often more interesting than one that leaves the characters sated and deliriously happy.

Sexual encounters are a chance for your characters to make connections or fail to make them. The needier they are to connect, the more interesting their disappointment and its aftermath can be. The shock of dashed expectations can (and perhaps should) lead characters to have insights, even epiphanies, about matters much broader than the condition of their genitals. This is certainly the case in examples I discuss later in the book from Erica Jong's *Fear of Flying* and John Lonie's short story "Contact."

Often the gulf between a lover's expectations and the reality of the encounter spark humor. In our interview, Edmund White pointed out that realistic sex scenes are often comic, "because the spirit outstrips the body." He elaborated:

> Henri Bergson defined humor as that thing that happens when the material world resists the spiritual world. In other words, two lovers want to leave for their honeymoon and they go out the revolving door and the door sticks. That's like the beginning of every *I Love Lucy* episode. In the same way, I think sex is a classic site for that kind of humor, because people have all kinds of extremely erotic ideas or romantic or passionate ideas about what they're going to accomplish in bed and oftentimes it's a fizzle. So that's part of the humor.

Perhaps the most interesting literary category of "unsatisfying sex" is sex that satisfies physically but leaves the lovers angry, empty, still yearning, or unequally fulfilled when it's over. See the discussions of *Before and After*, *Blue Angel*, and *Slow Dancing*.

3. It's okay—*really!*—to be aroused by your own writing.
If it's good enough for John Updike, it's good enough for the rest of us. "Writing my sex scenes physically excites me, as it should," he said. Jerome Badanes echoes this in discussing the graphic sex scenes in his novel, *The Final Opus of Leon Solomon*: "One way to make sure it's sexy—the first way—is to make sure I find it sexy." This does not mean that a good sex scene is just the writer's let-it-rip sexual fantasy. Far from it. Badanes again: "Sex scenes should not be advertisements for oneself." They should, as we stress in

other sections of this book, issue from character, deepen our involvement in the story, and/or fuel the plot. None of that means they can't be arousing, too.

4. Your fear is your best friend.

When I asked Dorothy Allison what advice she gives students on writing about sex in their fiction, the power of her answer led me to make this a basic principle. Here's what she said:

> I believe that fear is useful. . . . Remember when you played a game when you were a kid and you'd be looking for something and somebody would know where it was and they'd say, You're warm, you're warm, you're hot, you're cold! You've gone the wrong way. The fear works that way. What you are most afraid of is where the energy will flow the strongest, and for a writer, if you write in that direction, toward where the fear is, it's like a homing signal for what you need to do. . . .
>
> There's no safety in writing well. There is no way to be naked, which is what you have to be to be a good writer . . . and still be safe. . . . I think one of the things that's happened in sexual writing is we've gotten the notion that nakedness is about being explicit about details and techniques. I find that really tedious. What is truly naked is emotional exposure. And for every writer that's different. The place where you're pushing yourself the most emotionally is going to be different. It's way different for a lesbian than for a straight woman, it's way different depending on your age and the world you were brought up in, depending on who you're most afraid of, whether it's your family or those middle-class white girls who always made me so convinced they would spot me and throw me out. Every person has a fear. And your fear is your best friend.

5. Sex is nice, but character is destiny.

When I think of my favorite books, it is compelling characters, not plots, that come immediately to mind—characters or pairs of characters: Rosamund and Mr. Casaubon from George Eliot's *Middlemarch;* the fifteen-year-old French girl and her Chinese lover from Marguerite Duras's *The Lover;* the deluded narrator of Ford Madox Ford's *The Good Soldier.* Fiction without characters we care about is a dreary place to dwell.

What does this have to do with sex? Everything. We don't have to love your characters or trust them with our children, but if they don't engage us, we won't care even if they get lucky and find someone who wants to go to bed with them.

I need to care about your characters enough to care about their sex lives.

6. Only your characters know for sure (what to call it).

This is the question everyone wants the answer to: What do you call it? When he was writing his first novel, *Body and Soul,* Frank Conroy, the director of the University of Iowa's Writers' Workshop and author of a classic memoir, *Stop-Time,* told me that he dreaded having to write the sex scenes he knew were part of the story: "Do you say 'cock,' do you say 'prick'? Do you use all those words like 'slippery'?"

The narrator of Mary Gordon's sensual novel *Spending* puts the dilemma nicely: "Most words that connect up with sex have one kind of bad effect or another. Either I laugh or I want to become a Carmelite. Slang is no good. Scientific names are no good, either. They make me think I've been given a terminal diagnosis."

Edmund White points out that the French have a good, all-purpose word, *le verge,* for the male member, that is neither slang nor clinical; it does not call attention to itself the way our own choices do.

Though I cannot give you a list of *les mots justes* for every occasion, I offer these general guidelines:

- Call it what your characters would call it. If this happens to be slang that might be unfamiliar to your readers, or slang that sounds cute or out of character, establish that this word or these words are the accepted argot for this couple or in this circle.

- Whatever your choice, make sure it is appropriate to the tone of the book.
- Don't be cute and evasive—unless the characters are and you have established credible reasons for their attitudes.
- There is always clinical terminology, which may not win any prizes for poetry but will get you where you need to go without calling too much attention to itself.
- It may not be necessary to call it anything. In his novel *Paradise News*, discussed in chapter 3, David Lodge has written a sexy sex scene and circumvented any need to name names. Examples by Mary Gordon in chapter 5 and Ian McEwan in chapter 7 also smartly skirt the dilemma.

7. Take your cues from your characters.

Mickey Friedman, author of many mystery novels, admitted to me, "It's difficult to pin down what my characters should do when they drift toward the bedroom." Easy. Let your characters show you the way. Follow them into the bedroom, don't make them wait for instructions. If that advice still leaves you stuck in neutral in the living room, gaping at your befuddled couple, ignore one of them for a few minutes and focus all your loving, observant attention on the other. What does she want to happen—in the next ten minutes and in the next ten days? What else or who else does she have on her mind? Is there anything she is afraid of at the moment? If she were asked to describe what the man in her arms wants from her tonight, what would she say? If she were asked what he might want from her tomorrow morning, what would she say?

Once you can locate one character's state of mind and desire, turn your attention to her partner. How does he respond to her stated and unstated fears and needs?

When you decide it's time for your characters to hop into bed together, you may be pushing them to do something they are not

ready for or don't want as much as you want them to want it. How
will you know? See Principle #8.

8. Your characters must want and want intensely.

Whether your characters are moving toward the bedroom or the
Eiffel Tower, don't let them go too far without taking stock of
what they want—want in the next ten minutes and want as fictional entities in this universe they have helped you create. Novelist Janet Burroway explains this matter of "wanting" as an
elemental force in writing in her book *Writing Fiction*. Her words
apply to writing about sex and everything else:

> It is true that in fiction, in order to engage our attention and
> sympathy, the central character must want and want intensely.
> The thing that character wants need not be violent or spectacu-
> lar; it is the intensity of the wanting that counts. She may want
> only to survive, but if so she must want enormously to survive,
> and there must be distinct cause to doubt she will succeed.

If you do not know what to do when your characters drift
toward the bedroom, learn to recognize this uncertainty as one of
nature's warning signs that you need to check in with them, like a
doctor making rounds. Begin by making sure at least one character wants something out of the upcoming sexual encounter. But
whatever your character wants, remember that in fiction it is
always more interesting if he does not get what he wants, or gets
what he wants but finds it was not what he wanted after all, or has
to pay a heavy price for what he has gotten.

A character who wants something that his partner does not
want to give him is what dramatic conflict is all about. Some conflict leads to large-scale strife between characters; some is just verbal bantering that tells us about the nature of your characters'
intimacy. And some seemingly innocuous parrying can foreshadow more high-stakes drama yet to come. In the realm of

writing about sex, dramatic conflict can begin with no more than two characters who have different expectations for an afternoon rendezvous.

9. A good sex scene is always about sex and something else.

One of the rules of fiction writing is that the rules are meant to be broken, but here's one I've rarely found reason to tamper with: Make sure there are two things happening at once, whether you're writing dialogue or a sex scene. I don't mean there has to be sex and stamp collecting; I mean the sex needs a purpose in your story beyond the momentary frisson it brings to your characters. It needs to reveal something about them, act as a metaphor, a symbol, or an illustration of an aspect of your theme, your plot, and/or your characters' desires and dilemmas.

When I asked Russell Banks if there was a point in his career when he felt inhibited writing about sex and a moment when the inhibition lifted, he gave an answer that led to another example of the two-things-at-once principle:

> I don't think I ever felt particularly inhibited about it. I think when I first began writing I was less clear about the difference between writing and fantasizing, and so when I wrote about sex I tended to have a sexual fantasy. It took a while to realize that wasn't doing anyone any good, not even me, and it wasn't doing the writing any good. I began to realize I had to approach it with the same attention to craft and to function in the larger work that I did with every other scene. . . .
>
> There is a scene in *Continental Drift* when [my main character] Bob Dubois is having sex and imagines himself at a boat landing on the shore of the New World, skimming up over the beach with the waves forcing him forward, which is meant to be a slight parody of the conventions of sex writing, where they always invoke waves and tides and things like that. And also a slight parody of the unconscious sexist language used to

describe "the New World." Since this fit with some of the themes of the book, I thought it was useful to do. And I lost complete contact with whether or not it was good for Bob— because I was having so much fun relating the sex to all these other things and using it in other ways. At that point I realized what a powerful and wonderful metaphor a sex scene can be in a story, for things utterly other than sex. How you could use a sex scene to develop and dramatize themes in the book that had nothing to do with sex. . . . This was when I began to realize the literary possibilities of a sex scene and didn't just use it either sentimentally or to indulge myself in a sexual fantasy.

Sex in real life doesn't have to be about anything but sex, but in fiction it has to reveal something about who the characters are, what they want, what they might not get, what they think they can get away with, or what this collision of bodies has to do with everything that comes before and after in your story.

10. Who your characters are to each other is key.
Have your literary lovers been married for thirty years? Have they just met? Are they old friends? There is no more important element in crafting a sex scene than the relationship between sex partners. It is so crucial that in this book chapters 5 through 11 are devoted to exploring the nature of specific sexual relationships and how writers can learn to combine the general truths about them with the particular circumstances of their characters and their stories. In the meantime, go on to chapter 3 for a few more general principles that are beyond the basics.

3

BEYOND THE BASICS: "SURPRISE ME" AND OTHER LITERARY COME-ONS

> The trick is, of course, once sex is not off-limits, to keep it
> from being boring, and to make it continuous with the
> book's psychology and symbolism elsewhere.
>
> —JOHN UPDIKE,
> letter to author

Many of the earlier principles introduced you to the idea of focusing on your characters' whole selves and relationships to each other rather than on their body parts as you feel their way through a sex scene. The principles presented in this chapter focus on the more technical aspects of *how* to make these characters and relationships come alive and do all the things you need them to do for your story—chief among them, to keep us from being bored by a sex scene that's all plumbing. These are the principles we will be exploring and learning to apply here:

1. Sex is not an ATM withdrawal.
2. Hire a decorator.

3. Your characters don't have to speak to each other, but don't forget that they can.
4. You need not be explicit, but you must be specific.
5. Surprise me.

1. Sex is not an ATM withdrawal.

Narrate from inside your characters' bodies and minds, not from a camera set up to record the transaction. If you are writing about a Peeping Tom, his experience of sex-from-a-distance is exactly what you should be describing. But if your character is in bed with another character or two, put us right there with at least one of them. Whatever else it is, sex is a physical experience, and part of your job is, in some way, to make those sensations immediate and accessible to the reader. This does not mean you must file a report on every twitch. Nor does it mean you should limit your observations to the feel of flesh against flesh. In addition to unruly memories and unbidden thoughts, people have eyes, ears, and noses, each with a highly specialized and sensitive job to perform. Anaïs Nin described this orchestra of senses in her diary: "There are so many minor senses, all running like tributaries into the mainstream of sex, nourishing it."

To sharpen your awareness of your senses and to discover a language in which to write about them, read Diane Ackerman's sensuous and learned study *A Natural History of the Senses* (Vintage paperback). As a poet and dedicated sensualist, she offers a history and appreciation of the senses so rich you may come to believe your nose is the most important part of your body, except for your eyes and ears.

2. Hire a decorator.

Most of the principles we've looked at have focused on setting the emotional stage, creating characters who are fully developed enough that we can care about their sex lives along with the rest of their lives, and so that the sex scenes relate to the larger story. But to really deliver the moment, as Jerome Badanes puts it, we also need to see them in their physical surroundings, whether they are in a hammock or the Lincoln Room in the White House. What your characters see around them is as important as what they feel and remember.

Once they begin to disrobe, make them as aware of their physical surroundings as they are when they are not making love. Create a connection between their physical surroundings, their relationship, and the larger concerns of the story. John Casey does this beautifully in his novel *Spartina*, about a Rhode Island fisherman, Dick Pierce, in love with his wife, his lover Elsie, and the fishing boat called *Spartina* that he is determined to build and then has to save heroically when a hurricane threatens to destroy it. In a scene where he and Elsie make love at night along the banks of a salt marsh, the physical details of their bodies become almost indistinguishable from those of the surroundings, because the point of view is Dick's and he is thoroughly in touch with the natural world. He even compares Elsie at orgasm to a fish:

> He turned his head so his cheek was flat against her. He could feel her muscles moving softly—her coming was more in her mind still; when she got closer she would become a single band of muscle, like a fish—all of her would move at once, flickering and curving, unified from jaw to tail. . . . After a while they moved up the bank as though they had to escape the flood. They clambered onto the table of higher ground, onto the spartina. . . . He got his feet out of his pants and made a bed of them for her on the long flattened stalks.

Whether your characters are making love in a salt marsh or between pink satin sheets in a Pocono honeymoon hotel, use the physical surroundings the same way a set designer does in a play: to create a mood, to reveal information about who the characters are, and to make the actors moving across the stage as real to us as people in your living room.

3. Your characters don't have to speak, but don't forget that they can.

The subtitle to this section is *not* Talk Dirty to Me. There is—or should be—a lot more to dialogue between literary lovers than that. Words, Anaïs Nin writes in her diary, "carry colors and sounds into the flesh." When you allow your characters to speak to each other, you can bottle some of that erotic power and add conflict, intrigue, tenderness, just about any emotion you want, to your sex scenes. There is nothing like good dialogue to draw us into the world of the book, straight into bed with your characters, which is exactly where you want us to be.

In sex scenes, dialogue can have four important functions:

1. It reveals information about who characters are.
2. The information dialogue reveals can create conflict between characters or clue us in on the conflict between the lovers and the outside world, as happens in adulterous or other forbidden sex.
3. Through dialogue, characters can explore and resolve conflicts, or realize they will not be able to resolve them.
4. Dialogue can reveal your characters' attitudes toward sex and sexuality, which often affects the course and outcome of a sex scene.

All four functions are at work in this passage from British writer David Lodge's novel *Paradise News*, a serious comedy about sexual awakening, religious faith, and the Hawaiian tourist industry. Bernard, a forty-one-year-old virgin and former man of the cloth in Hawaii visiting his dying aunt, gets lessons in love from a vibrant divorcée named Yolande, who is a mental health counselor. They have been meeting for several afternoons in his hotel, and because he is so afraid of sex, she has been introducing him to it slowly, a little each day.

Tomorrow there was more light in the room, and they split a half-bottle of white wine from the minibar before they began. Yolande was bolder and far more loquacious. "Today is still touching only, but nowhere is off-limits, we can touch where we like, how we like, OK? And it needn't be just hands, you can also use your mouth and your tongue. Would you like to suck my breasts? Go ahead. Is that nice? Good, it's nice for me. Can I suck you? Don't worry, I'll squeeze it hard like this and that'll stop you coming. OK. Relax. Was that nice? Good. Sure I like to do it. Sucking and licking are very primal pleasures. Of course, it's easy to see what pleases a man, but with women it's different, it's all hidden inside and you've got to know your way around, so lick your finger, and I'll give you the tour."

He was shocked, bemused, almost physically winded by this sudden acceleration into a tabooless candor of word and gesture. But he was elated too. He hung on for dear life. "Are we going to make love today?" he pleaded.

"This is making love, Bernard," she said. "I'm having a wonderful time, aren't you?"

"Yes, but you know what I mean."

What does dialogue do for this scene?

It's funny and fun to read. It pulls the reader as close to the action as the characters are. It delineates the differences between these two characters and thereby creates just enough gentle conflict to hold our interest and get us involved in the mild struggle between them. In a reversal of the traditional roles, Yolande is experienced and comfortable—the aggressor. Bernard, overwhelmed by her bluntness and know-how, can only sputter a few words. Their speech reveals who they are and that they are coming to this event with vastly different experience and expectations.

Most cleverly, the dialogue, and particularly Yolande's monologue, make it possible to eliminate clunky sexual stage directions, saving us, the characters, and the author the awkward business of "What do you call it?" Had Lodge used a step-by-step format, bits of dialogue followed by stage directions—e.g., "She held his penis in her hand and said, 'Sometimes people suck them,' and bent her head down to his . . ."—the results would have been excruciating. As is, we are charmed, amused, and maybe a little turned on by forthright Yolande. We probably have some empathy, and maybe a touch of envy, for Bernard, who has no idea what is happening and no idea how much fun he is about to have.

Dialogue should reveal aspects of character, particularly as they relate to how people express, or have difficulty expressing, their sexuality.

The talking that leads up to sex is often more interesting to read about and write about than the thing itself, because there are more possibilities for intrigue and for the unexpected. This is the case in Don DeLillo's *White Noise,* a dark comedy of American "magic and dread," as husband and wife prepare for bed by discussing what erotic literature they will read that night. Their dialogue satirizes both married sex and the "he entered her" school of erotic writing. The husband, Jack, professor of Hitler studies at a midwestern university, narrates:

> I said, "Pick your century. Do you want to read about Etruscan slave girls, Georgian rakes? I think we have some literature on flagellation brothels. What about the Middle Ages? We have incubi and succubi. Nuns galore."
>
> "Whatever's best for you."
>
> "I want you to choose. It's sexier that way. . . ."
>
> "I will read," she said. "But I don't want you to choose anything that has men inside women, quote-unquote, or men entering women. 'I entered her.' 'He entered me.' We're not lobbies or elevators. 'I wanted him inside me,' as if he could crawl completely in, sign the register, sleep, eat, so forth. Can we agree on that? I don't care what these people do as long as they don't enter or get entered."

"Agreed."

"'I entered her and began to thrust.'"

"I'm in total agreement."

"'Enter me, enter me, yes, yes.'"

"Silly usage, absolutely."

"'Insert yourself, Rex. I want you inside me, entering hard, entering deep, yes, now, oh.'"

I began to feel an erection stirring. How stupid and out of context. Babette laughed at her own lines. . . .

In this passage, the dialogue is used to create and resolve a conflict between the characters. Babette insists they read nothing that has "men inside women." Though Jack agrees and says so, the conflict arises when Babette humorously continues to insist, while Jack continues to agree. The result is that Babette gets to say a lot of silly erotic things that she actually finds objectionable, and which ironically have the effect of arousing her husband—the purpose of the erotic readings in the first place. The conflict is resolved in the last paragraph, with Jack aroused and Babette laughing.

Dialogue between lovers need not take place *in bed*. A prelude to a sex scene can tell us more about the nature of your lovers' sexual relationship than a home video.

Dialogue need not be extensive to convey your characters' ardor and attitudes. In this brief passage from Alice Walker's *The Color Purple*, Celie, a poor, uneducated, mistreated young woman, mother and stepmother to many, has her first truly intimate, loving sexual experience with a confident woman named Shug. The novel is in the form of Celie's letters to God, addressing God because she has no one else in whom to confide. Shug has been staying with Celie and her casually brutal husband, Albert, who is also Shug's lover. One night when Albert is away, Shug and Celie share a bed and Celie confides the sorrows of her life to Shug, a recitation that ends like this:

Nobody ever love me, I say.

She say, I love you, Miss Celie. And then she haul off and kiss me on the mouth.

Um, she say, like she surprise. I kiss her back, say, *um,* too. Us kiss and kiss till us can't hardly kiss no more. Then us touch each other.

I don't know nothing bout it, I say to Shug.

I don't know much, she say.

Then I feels something real soft and wet on my breast, feel like one of my little lost babies mouth.

Way after while, I act like a little lost baby too.

Earlier, Celie had told Shug she hated sex with her husband, that he never tried to please her—and they never talked about any of it. The fact that Celie feels safe enough to say anything to Shug represents a breakthrough for her. The limited dialogue in this passage keeps the focus on the intimacy between the two women and on their mutual discovery of this new kind of sex. When Celie says to us, "Then us touch each other," and says to Shug, "I don't know nothing bout it," we get a vivid sense of the mood of the moment, Celie's nervousness and anticipation, and the comfort and safety she feels for the first time in her life.

4. You need not be explicit, but you must be specific.

"Sex almost always disappoints me in novels," a well-read psychiatrist told the late critic Anatole Broyard, in a column in the *New York Times*. "Everything can be said or done now, and that's what I often find: everything, a feeling of generality or dispersal. But in my experience, true sex is so particular, so peculiar to the person who yearns for it. Only he or she, and no one else, would desire so very much that very person under those circumstances. In fiction, I miss that sense of terrific specificity."

This idea is expressed in more colloquial language in Scott Turow's recent novel, *Personal Injuries.* "Sex is always strange," the main character tries to assure a younger woman who is self-conscious about her sexuality. "I mean, this is the most private, inner thing in life, isn't it? . . . It comes out just a little bit differently in each of us, like a fingerprint. Who you do what with. And your fantasies. And what part you like best. And what you're thinking. It's unique. That's why it's intimate. That's why it's magic."

The specific is what makes you fall in love with one person instead of another. It's what makes walking through the Amazon rain forest different from walking through the California redwoods, though tall trees are present in both. It's what makes a four-star restaurant different from the neighborhood pub, and William Faulkner different from Eudora Welty, though they are both from Mississippi.

You create specificity through details, whether they are details that distinguish one character's dialogue from another or that describe emotion, action, a landscape, or the feel of mosquitoes buzzing around your main character's recently pierced earlobe the August night he loses his virginity in Yellowstone National Park by the light of a full moon.

Though the two are often confused in writing about sex, being specific is different from being explicit. Pornography, in most cases, is an extreme example of the explicit without the specific. It gives us a twitch-by-twitch account of who put what where, with a focus on the welfare and whereabouts of everyone's genitals. It almost never reveals anything that distinguishes one pair of lovers from another, except perhaps in the measurement of sex organs or physical sensations.

Specificity—to time, place, and cultural and geographical circumstances—abounds in this scene from *The Mambo Kings Play Songs of Love*, Oscar Hijuelos's melodious novel about a pair of brothers, Cuban immigrants, who become stars of New York's Latino dance halls in the 1950s. From the present day, brother Cesar Castillo is reminiscing about that period, when he and his brother called themselves "the Mambo Kings," in honor of the music they played. Note how Hijuelos incorporates both music and geography (of special interest to immigrants) into this love scene between Castillo and Vanna Vane, a cigarette girl he met in a club. They have just made love, during which "he pumped her so much he tore up the rubber and kept going." A little later the same night:

Smugly, he showed her his *pinga*, as it was indelicately called in his youth. He was sitting on the bed in the Hotel Splendour and leaning back in the shadows, while she was standing by the bathroom door. And just looking at her fine naked body, damp with sweat and happiness, made his big thing all hard again. That thing burning in the light of the window was thick and dark as a tree branch. In those days, it sprouted like a vine from between his legs, carried aloft by a powerful vein that precisely divided his body, and flourished upwards like the spreading top branches of a tree, or, he once thought while looking at a map of the United States, like the course of the Mississippi River and its tributaries.

"Come over here," he told her.

On that night, as on many other nights, he pulled up the tangled sheets so that she could join him on the bed again. And soon Vanna Vane was grinding her damp bottom against his chest, belly, and mouth and strands of her dyed blond hair came slipping down between their lips as they kissed. Then she mounted him and rocked back and forth until things got all twisted and hot inside and both their hearts burst (pounding like conga drums) and they fell back exhausted, resting until they were ready for more, their lovemaking going around and around in the Mambo King's head, like the melody of a song of love.

How does Hijuelos achieve specificity in this scene?

- He uses an abundance and variety of details to locate Cesar at that youthful, fecund, and exciting time of his life. By pointing out twice that all this happened "in those days," he is saying by inference that he is no longer as young, strong, or sexually active.

• There is a strong single point of view (Cesar's) through which everything is observed, felt, and remembered.

• This celebrated maker of mambo music experiences sex through musical metaphors. Their hearts don't pound like just any drums but like "conga drums." The rhythms of the sentences, particularly the last sentence, are lush and exuberant and suggest an openness to sensation and emotion that is also characteristic of mambo music.

• Cesar's status as a recent arrival is reinforced by his comparing the vein of his penis to a tributary of the Mississippi River. While anyone might reasonably study a map, a newcomer is likely to look at it with fresh eyes and a greater sense of wonder than someone more familiar with the country.

• The detail of Vanna Vane's dyed blond hair, mentioned in this passage only in passing, becomes an important characteristic several paragraphs later. Cesar remembers that in those days "to be seen with a woman like Vanna was prestigious as a passport, a high school diploma, a full-time job, a record contract, a 1951 DeSoto." Immigrants hungry for this kind of prestige will take—or will have to settle for—a dyed blonde, not the real thing. Just as Cesar knows he is not a "Real American," Vanna is not a Real Blonde.

In a much less sexually explicit scene in a short story by fiction writer and physician Ethan Canin, "We Are Nighttime Travelers," an elderly husband and wife estranged for many years—"There have been three presidents since I held her in my arms"—rediscover each other. The husband narrates.

I do not say anything. Instead I roll in the bed, reach across, and touch her, and because she is surprised she turns to me.

When I kiss her the lips are dry, cracking against mine, unfamiliar as the ocean floor. But then the lips give. They part. I am inside her mouth, and there, still hidden from the world, as if ruin had forgotten a part, it is wet—Lord! I have the feeling of a miracle. Her tongue comes forward. I do not know myself then, what man I am, who I lie with in embrace. I can barely remember her beauty. She touches my chest and I bite lightly on her lip, spread moisture to her cheek and then kiss there. She makes something like a sigh. "Frank," she says. "Frank." We are lost now in seas and deserts. My hand finds her fingers and grips them, bone and tendon, fragile things.

Without knowing much more about these characters, this brief, complete, and very specific description, exclusively from the husband's point of view, tells us a great deal about who they are: elderly, fragile, once intimate, and more excited and tenderly disposed than either might have expected. The husband's feelings of expansiveness at this moment are conveyed in part through metaphors about the ocean floor, seas and deserts, places so vast and elemental that they suggest immeasurable depth and history, which could parallel the history of a marriage. Particularly moving is the wife's eagerness and the husband's joyous but silent surprise as he encounters it.

Whether your lovers are young and randy or old and infirm, their familiar journey toward sexual connection should be anything but predictable, in large measure because you create it using details and a voice that are specific to *these* characters at *this* particular moment in their lives and in the story.

5. Surprise me.

In real life, we generally enjoy the company of congenial people, but when we read literature, we often prefer characters who are difficult, vexing, selfish, self-involved, diabolical, ambitious, vain—complex creations who cause themselves and those around them trouble. The trouble can be as vast and destructive as Captain Ahab's obsession with the whale in *Moby Dick*, or as quietly irksome as Bartleby's refusal to say anything other than "I would prefer not to," in Melville's haunting short story, "Bartleby the Scrivener."

But whether our characters' demons are internal or external, whether they are extraordinary people or ordinary people faced with extraordinary challenges, we are drawn to the conflict that swirls around them. On an emotional level it engages our curiosity and possibly our sympathy, if not for the most difficult characters then for their victims. On a technical level, the conflict created by these characters helps move the story forward. What will he do next? we wonder. How will he get out of *this* one? we ask ourselves and keep turning the pages. The most compelling characters in fiction are often their own worst enemies: they antagonize, alienate, throw metaphorical bricks through metaphorical windows. Or real snowballs that set in motion a series of accidents, births, and deaths that occupy Robertson Davies's characters throughout his best-known long work, *The Deptford Trilogy.*

But whether their gestures are large or small, whether they are victims or perpetrators, whether, as T. S. Eliot says, "they murder or create," the best characters continually surprise us, even if it is only with their own stubbornness. And they continually create conflict for themselves and everyone in their midst.

When you lead your characters into bed together, these same dynamics must happen in miniature. When writing about these few intimate moments, which are not generally characterized by conflict, you must nevertheless create some kind of conflict, tension, or surprise, whether it is in the language, the relationship between the characters, the relationship between a pair of lovers and the hostile outside world, or between a narrator and the lovers whose story you are telling, as happens in James Salter's highly erotic novel, *A Sport and a Pastime* (discussed in chapter 8).

There are few if any surprises in pornography: everything moves inexorably toward the orgasm. A well-written sex scene manages to rewrite pornography's punch line so that we remember not the force of the characters' orgasms but the thing that happened that we didn't expect, what I'm calling The Surprise. The Surprise, though, is not a single, discrete entity. Good writing offers all kinds of surprises and pleasures—of scene, plot, character, and language—and good writing about sex does, too.

Most readers, I imagine, were startled by this very brief scene about halfway into the popular Danish thriller by Peter Høeg, *Smilla's Sense of Snow*, which Smilla, a female sleuth, narrates:

> Standing in the middle of the bedroom, we take off each other's clothes.
>
> He has a light, fumbling brutality, which several times makes me think that this time it'll cost me my sanity. In our dawning, mutual intimacy, I induce him to open the little slit in the head of his penis so I can put my clitoris inside and fuck him.

With that eerie multiple role reversal (the author is a man), the chapter ends. The unusual physical connection is indeed a surprise to us, but it is not a gratuitous surprise because it fits with Smilla's character: she has renounced the traditional passive female role, whether she's investigating a crime or falling in love.

Another brief, startlingly sexy surprise can be found in Raj Kamal Jha's haunting and sad first novel, *The Blue Bedspread*, published in 1999. Young lovers in Calcutta who have nowhere else to be intimate go to the movie theater. The woman wears a skirt; they sit in the back row.

> As the credits begin to roll, my fingers move up her leg. Her skin, smooth up to where she rubbed the cream after her bath. By the time the music director's name appears on the screen, I can feel her legs clench, her legs give way.
>
> I slide my fingers deep, through the warmth, through the wetness. And when they slip in, I write I L-O-V-E Y-O-U on the inner wall inside her, letter by letter. By the time I reach the second O, she's trembling.

Moving to a much larger canvas, one of the most erotically charged sexual encounters in all of literature, in *Madame Bovary*, has its own unique surprise: in it we see nothing at all of the impassioned lovers, only the horse-drawn carriage that thunders through the streets of nineteenth-century Rouen, shuddering, propelled by the force of the lovemaking unleashed inside it.

Let's look at some of the more ordinary surprises good writers spring on us, often so subtly we aren't aware of it, in order to give depth and texture to their sex scenes. This list covers broad categories, and clearly some examples are appropriate for more than one category. In your own reading and writing, you will certainly encounter other kinds of surprises.

THE SURPRISE OF ACTION. In which something occurs that shifts our attention away from the orgasm or from the mechanics of sex. The action or occurrence might be as dramatic as a cuckolded husband leaping out of a bedroom closet at the moment of truth or as inert as a wife falling asleep while her husband makes love to her, as in John Updike's *Rabbit Is Rich*.

THE SURPRISE OF SPEECH. In which characters speak while making love, which again can shift the focus away from the predictable mechanics of sex. As with all good dialogue, dialogue in this setting should be there for a reason integral to the characters and the story. We should learn something about the characters or their circumstances from what they say to each other in bed. In Scott Turow's *Presumed Innocent*, narrator Rusty Sabitch remembers his torrid, illicit affair with Carolyn Polhemus, whose murder he is accused of committing. In recounting their sex life, he tells us that she used to "roam, take my penis in her mouth, let it go, and slide her hand past my scrotum, probing in that hole." Then she would cruelly ask, "'Does Barbara [his wife] do this for you?'" Rusty understood her comment to be a manipulative and disarming play in their power struggle, leaving Rusty humiliated and exposed. Carolyn, he tells us, "could bring my wife into our bed and make her one more witness to how much I was willing to abandon." Later, when Carolyn invites Rusty to make love to her anally, she repeats the line, "Does Barbara do this for you?" which reveals her skill at manipulating and controlling him by exploiting the shame he feels for betraying his wife.

THE SURPRISE OF DISTRACTION. A character becomes distracted by something or someone. The noise of a child upstairs; a lover's tears; a memory; a nearby object; a disturbing thought.

THE SURPRISE OF INSIGHT. In which a description of a sexual encounter includes an insight or important observation, as when Rusty Sabitch admits that "after seventeen years of faithful marriage, of wandering impulse suppressed for the sake of tranquil domestic life, I could not believe that I was here, with fantasy made real . . . in the land beyond restraint, rescued from the diligent, slowly moving circles of my life. Each time I entered [Carolyn], I felt I divided the world."

THE SURPRISE OF LANGUAGE. Because we create with language, not oil paint and not stone, the necessary surprise need not involve an unexpected turn of events but only an unexpected turn of phrase. Our goal should not be cleverness or verbal contrivance but original language and metaphor that demand our attention, words that are particularly eloquent in doing what our words are meant to do: move the reader to feel what the character feels at that moment, whether it is arousal, excitement, melancholy, fear, or revulsion. The surprise of language at its most eloquent, inventive, and/or metaphorical forces the reader to think about sex in a way she has not before, as when James Salter, in *A Sport and a Pastime,* says of the lovers Dean and Anne-Marie: "He kisses her side and then, without force, as one stirs a favorite mare, begins again. She comes to life with a soft, exhausted sound, like someone saved from drowning." Later in the novel, as they make love, "She begins to roll her hips, to cry out. It's like ministering to a lunatic."

In this description from *Written on the Body* by English novelist Jeanette Winterson, we are very conscious of the presence of the writer—the creator of these many metaphors—but far from distancing the reader, the vividness and aptness of the metaphors and the active involvement of the "I" lure us into the narrator's rich sexual and sensory life. Note the enlarging movement in the metaphors from animals (cats and horses) to sea life and finally to the tides, which suggest sensual, undulating movement, and the predictable, repetitive cycles we find both in lust and in nature.

> She arches her body like a cat on a stretch. She nuzzles her cunt into my face like a filly at the gate. She smells of the sea. She smells of rockpools when I was a child. She keeps a starfish in there. I crouch down to taste the salt, to run my fingers around the rim. She opens and shuts like a sea anemone. She's refilled each day with fresh tides of longing.

In a very different example, the language is so stark and stripped down it comes close to dispensing with the illusion that we are reading an account. In this scene from "Home," an early piece by novelist and short fiction writer Jayne Anne Phillips, I feel so close to the narrator and the dream she relates that I flinch every time I read it. She is a recent college graduate living reluctantly with her aging, divorced mother. Though the young woman has had lovers, she has never had an orgasm. She remembers having a dream:

> My father comes to me in a dream. He kneels beside me, touches my mouth. He turns my face gently toward him.
> Let me see, he says. Let me see it.
> He is looking for a scar, a sign. He wears only a towel around his waist. He presses himself against my thigh, pretending solicitude. But I know what he is doing; I turn my head in repulsion and stiffen. He smells of sour musk and his forearms are black with hair. I think to myself, It's been years since he's had an erection—
> Finally he stands. Cover yourself, I tell him. I can't, he says, I'm hard.

The scene ends there, with a patch of white space, the words "I'm hard" hanging ominously in the air, leaving us as disturbed as the narrator is by this dream. Though she never tells us whether the dream reenacts scenes of genuine abuse, we sense a sexual disturbance in the household, a hint as to her failure to have satisfying sexual relationships. The language of the scene is so straightforward it feels more as if we are experiencing this event—dreaming this dream—ourselves.

What is interesting emotionally about this dream is that it is not the simple account of aggressor and victim. Most compelling is not the father's approach to the girl or her turning him away, but what happens *after* she turns him away. Far from expressing distaste for what has happened, although we know she feels it, she becomes more of an adult participant, less of a victim, when she thinks: "It's been years since he's had an erection." Rather than telling him to get out of her room or out of her life—a wholesale rejection—she equivocates: "Cover yourself," as if to say, "I want you to stay, but I don't want to see more evidence of your desire right now." By not rejecting him outright, she is, in some sense, acknowledging her own desire and arousal. This is as disturbing to her and to us as the father's violation.

SURPRISE PLATTER. Philip Roth's succès de scandale, *Portnoy's Complaint*, includes a scene that touches on every possible kind of surprise known to young men and writers. Teenage Alex Portnoy, who is totally obsessed with masturbation, goes with a group of friends to visit a prostitute, having been told by the boy who arranged the trip that they will all "get laid."

Far from losing his virginity, young Portnoy ends up with a tired hooker named Bubbles who is ready to go home. She refuses to do anything but masturbate him. Once she begins and sees it might take a while—"It is like trying to jerk off a jellyfish," he confesses—she ups the stakes and says he has only fifty seconds in which to finish. The only way he can manage to arouse himself is by fantasizing about masturbating. But when he is finally at the

point of orgasm, she says, "'Okay, that's it . . . fifty,' *and stops!*"
He begs for another few seconds. "'Look, I already ironed two
hours, you know, before you guys even got here—'" She will not
give in. "Whereupon, unable (as always) to stand the frustration—the deprivation and disappointment—I reach down, I grab
it, and POW!" Not only is he reduced to doing it himself—"I ask
you, who jerks me off as well as I do it myself?"—but suffers
another indignity when "the jet . . . lands with a thick wet burning splash right in my own eye."

Almost every line of this scene serves up something unexpected, and the stakes keep rising higher and higher. "Son of a
bitch kike," Bubbles screams. "You got gissum all over the couch!
And the walls! And the lamp!" Portnoy is not only worried about
the possibility of going blind—but about the personal and historical implications of being called a kike. And on and on it goes.
Roth manages to turn the cliché of the teenage boy's first visit to a
whore into a rich, side-splittingly funny scene that leads us back
again to the themes of the novel, the struggle between being a
good Jew and a good Jewish son and being as naughty as your
libido begs you to be.

Writing about sex presents a panoply of challenges to all fiction
writers. The arrival of AIDS into our lives has forced a sea change
in sexual behavior and attitudes and has had a profound effect on
what many of us write about when we write about sex these days.
In the next chapter, we will take a look at some of new literary
challenges AIDS requires of us.

4

2001 VS. 1995: TWO VIEWS OF WRITING ABOUT SEX IN THE AGE OF AIDS

AIDS has killed more than 438,000 Americans and nearly 22 million people worldwide since . . . June 5, 1981. In this country, the disease control agency estimates, as many as 900,000 people are infected with H.I.V. . . . Each year, federal health officials say, another 40,000 Americans become infected with H.I.V. Globally, the figure was 5.3 million last year.

> —*New York Times*,
> "AIDS at 20," June 3, 2001

Dates matter in this discussion. I'm revising this chapter during the week that marks the twentieth year since the first official news reports about what came to be called AIDS. The newspapers and airwaves are full of numbers, projections, interviews, history, summaries of the bad news, and what little there is in the way of good news. But the main news, in 2001, is that AIDS is an inescapable fact of life and is no longer the death sentence it once was. When we read the sentence, "AIDS has changed nearly everything about America," which appeared recently in the *New York Times*, even those of us who are not infected and do not live in "high-risk" communities can explain in some detail what has changed. Six years ago, when I wrote the first version of this chapter, I might not have put the phrase "high-risk" in quotes, because at the time there was a clearer sense of division and separateness between those who were at risk and those who were not. There is a more pervasive understanding today that all communities are at risk, and that each one of us is at risk—if not of becoming infected ourselves, then of knowing someone who is, a child, sibling, parent, or friend.

The AIDS-aware fiction I read when preparing to write the first edition was full of grief, rage, and astonishment at the horror and dimensions of the disease—at the fact of the disease itself. Though there is no less grief in more recent fiction, a combination of exposure, resignation, and breakthrough advances in drug treatments have tempered some of the high notes, varied the tone, and made room for other narratives to exist in concert with the once predictable disease-driven trajectory.

Though H.I.V. and AIDS have affected tens of millions of people worldwide and a vast, varied assortment of Americans, their ravages have been chronicled in our fiction predominantly, almost exclusively, by gay white men. (For this reason, I have separated writing about gay and straight encounters. Following the two gay examples on pages 76 and 77, I turn my attention to fiction involving straight sexual encounters.) Not only did AIDS affect that community initially and devastatingly, but, in contrast to other affected groups—drug users, minorities, and the poor—white gays are affluent and educated, society's likeliest scribes. The outpouring has created a distinct genre, the literature of AIDS, which is inextricably intertwined with all of gay writing, as the literature of the Holocaust is fused with the history and literature of Jews in the twentieth century.

Sexual behavior has been an essential element in gay fiction, an expression of liberation encouraged by the Stonewall uprising and the larger sexual and political revolutions of the 1960s and 1970s. The appearance of AIDS has made explicit writing about sex even more relevant than it was as an act of rebellion and celebration of the new freedoms.

Because AIDS is a sexually transmitted disease, and because personal behavior plays the role it does, the politics and passions the subject generates are explosive, in real life and in fiction, inside and outside the gay community.

Controversy erupted when Saul Bellow published *Ravelstein*, a fictional homage to his friend Allan Bloom, the University of Chicago scholar and author of *The Closing of the American Mind*, who died in 1992, apparently of AIDS. Bellow's book was the first public acknowledgment of Bloom's homosexuality. The Ravelstein character urged the narrator-writer to tell his story when he was gone, but even Bloom's supposed complicity in "outing" himself did not prevent conservatives from feeling uneasy that one of their heroes was a gay victim of AIDS. Even with Bloom's blessing, some felt that Bellow had violated his privacy.

Within the gay community, blood was spilled when Larry Kramer, author, playwright, and activist, wrote a long essay, "Sex and Sensibility," in *The Advocate* (May 27, 1997), exhorting gay writers and artists to "create a new culture that is not confined and centered so tragically on our obsession with our penises and what we do with them." Acknowledging that what he was saying was "politically incorrect," Kramer said he was "sick of the literature of sex" and condemned Edmund White's then just-published novel, *The Farewell Symphony,* as "irresponsible," because of what he called the "faceless, indistinguishable pieces of flesh that litter these 500 pages." He went on to say, "It is impossible for me to believe that this book embodies what AIDS really represents to Edmund or that this is the kind of tribute he wishes to leave all his dead friends and lovers, or indeed, that this is all that becoming our most esteemed and respected writer has meant to him."

In our interview, Edmund White told me that he felt betrayed and misrepresented by Kramer in this essay. At the risk of entering the fray myself, I would argue that there is more to *The Farewell Symphony* than the narrator's sexual exploits: his luminous intelligence, rich wit, and Proustian perspicacity. The story is set in pre-AIDS New York in the 1970s and, as I read it, makes no pretenses to being either a tribute to White's dead friends and lovers or an embodiment of what AIDS represents to him. Several years later, White published *The Married Man,* a novel about the lingering death from AIDS of a Frenchman from the point of view of the lover who cared for him. It contains very little sex—and much discussion of the ascendancy of celibacy under these circumstances. Perhaps the politically correct book Kramer believed White should have written?

I say so much about this not to reignite the conflagration but to define the nature and intensity of these debates, because they reveal how much is at stake for gay men, personally and politically. Edmund White's comment from our interview illuminates other dimensions of the personal struggle:

> I bet there's very little gay sex that isn't shadowed by shame. I think AIDS brought that back into relief, because for those people who were just beginning to get finally adjusted to the idea that it was okay to be gay, AIDS came along and said, "No, you were right in the first place. Sex is dirty, it's a disease, you are wrong, it is against nature." AIDS really returned the adult gay man to his nerdy adolescence. It made you feel isolated, weird, as if you were really doing the wrong thing.

On the larger stage, because of AIDS, every act of gay sex and every piece of writing involving gay sex seem to stake out a political and moral position. Sympathy for gays runs higher when H.I.V. infection rates decline. Individuals judge and condemn others for their sexual choices: safe sex vs. unsafe; the steady lover vs. the bathhouse. Even the right to privacy—which in some fundamental sense is what gay liberation is about—is not an inalienable right, as revealed by the recent uproar over an article that exposed, or "outed," journalist Andrew Sullivan's Internet solicitations for unprotected sex. Sullivan's conservative politics and his prominent pieces in the *New York Times* and elsewhere have advocated gay marriage, condemned gay activists, and put forward the view—which many feel is highly irresponsible—that because of the new drug treatments, the worst of the AIDS crisis is over. Many feel that his own strident moralizing invited the "gotcha" journalism to which he became a victim.

What do all of these rumblings mean for those who write fiction involving gay sex? A great deal. Ironically, I believe the political and moral complexities of gay sexuality give the writer a clearer mandate of what can and should be expressed when writing a sex scene. "With gay sex," observes David Bergman, editor of the yearly *Men on Men* series of short fiction, "there's more of an obligation to write about the specifics, because there is no default position. There's no way ahead of time to know what the characters are going to do. How they handle it is all *so* loaded with the way we live now, you really have to explain it. Gay works of fiction that don't deal with it are cutting off experience."

Specifically:

- The characters' H.I.V. status is relevant, if not critical, information, which might be conveyed or implied long before the sex scene takes place.
- How the characters feel about their status and AIDS itself is relevant to the sex scene. Infected or uninfected, do they feel reckless, restrained, mournful—or all three?
- What emotional factors generate a character's sexual choices? What thoughts and actions are triggered when characters make decisions about how they intend to have sex and their plans change in midstream?

THE GAY COMMUNITY

These two very different examples suggest the range of choices writers have when writing about gay sexual encounters.

The tone of the stories in Andrew Holleran's collection, *In September, the Light Changes*, is, as the title suggests, pensive, quietly intense, and intensely luminous. Many stories touch on the upheaval that AIDS has wrought, though characters die offstage here, leaving survivors to ponder these two questions: "What will I do if/when I get sick? And: What will I do at sixty, if I don't?" ("Sunday Morning in Key West"). These stories are not heavy on sex, though they are infused with longing and the need for solace. In "Petunias" intimacy comes in a kiss.

Forty-four-year-old Morgan is back on Fire Island after an eight-year absence in the South and is given a job by a friend running a restaurant, where he falls in love with a young waiter. If there is nothing spectacular about the premise, the story's details, wit, and depth of feeling are out of the ordinary. Also out of the ordinary are Morgan's habits—he's celibate and sober after rehab and losing his New Orleans business to drink and tax troubles— and the habits of the young waiter, Ryan, who spends his free time either reading Thomas Mann in the grim waiters' sleeping quarters or visiting his grandmother on Long Island. The rest of gay Fire Island parties while the two men realize that they love to talk to each other. While they talk, Morgan pinches and plucks the dead leaves from the buckets of petunias on the deck, and the flowers begin to thrive, alerting others to their beauty and to the attachment developing between the two men.

One night they finally confront each other. "'My feelings for you have become inappropriate,'" Morgan tells him; there is a quaintness to the line in this land of sexual abandon. Ryan feels the same way. Their response—also unlikely by Fire Island standards:

They kissed and held each other for three hours. He kissed Ryan with all the pent-up desire and longing, the deprivation, the loneliness endured, the fear, the suffering of friends, the loss of almost everyone he loved, the joy that this was still possible, that it existed, that it was still there. . . . [H]e kissed him hungrily . . . with all his years of exile and depression, of faith destroyed and now revived.

Not long after, Morgan reports to his friend Girard that every night he and Ryan go back behind the restaurant and lie on a mat by the pool, kissing. Ryan doesn't want more than that. Girard's answer: " 'Welcome to the nineties!' "

The story works on the conflicts created by oppositions: older man, younger man; sobriety and celibacy on Fire Island; two grown-ups who do nothing but kiss. The beauty and fragility of the petunias echo the beauty and fragility of love. The first kiss has real meaning for Morgan: it's the first time in years he has felt comforted, felt his immense losses and burdens lifted.

The sexual ambience of William J. Mann's 1997 novel, *The Men from the Boys*, could not be further from the sun-drenched delicacy of "Petunias." It's a multigenerational story about families of origin and the families that gay men create as they struggle to define their lives and identities. Set in Boston and Provincetown in 1994 and 1995, narrator Jeff O'Brien is thirty-two years old and obsessed with the loss of sexual desirability that comes with age. He and live-in lover Lloyd tested negative for H.I.V. when they took the test together many years before. Each sleeps with others, the narrator with one-night or short-term "tricks." Lloyd, he says, prefers "meaningful encounters." "Lloyd finds the soul; I find the dick." One night at a Provincetown bar Jeff is rebuffed by a stranger, and after no one else approaches him he leaves the bar and goes looking for fun, Provincetown-style. He ends up in the sex spot of last resort, a place he has never been before, "the dick dock."

It's hard to see through the haze. Here, on the lip of the bay, it's like steam. . . . I can't even see the water. . . . Finally, I make out, not a foot away, a cluster of bodies, like a circle jerk among boys in their clubhouse. But in the middle of the circle is a man on his knees, moving with difficulty on the wet sand, cocks surrounding him like the spears of conquistadors—every faggot's dream, and don't let anyone ever tell you it's not.

I feel a hand on my crotch. I turn, confronted by a face. It's not unattractive, but it's hard to categorize. Old, young, I don't know. Montreal, New York, Boston—who cares? For in moments he's on his knees and my dick is out of my jeans, and he's sucking as fast as he can. He's high on something, I'm sure. . . . My dick swells now, ready to shoot. I attempt to withdraw, but he holds me there, and I come despite myself, ejaculating down his throat, the way I once did, more than ten years ago. . . .

It takes me a second to think, to quiet my heart in my ears. He *swallowed.* In ten years, that hasn't happened to me. I've always been so damned *good,* such a fucking role model, pulling out of the boys' mouths just before I came. That's how I was with Javitz, and Lloyd too: I have never tasted either's cum, and they have never tasted mine. Strange, isn't it, that this faceless man at the dick dock should have that part of me, and they don't? Maybe it's that generation thing again . . . for me, for Lloyd: we came out at the same time as the virus did, and were immediately bombarded with those hellish "safe sex" pamphlets that told us: *Do it and die.*

I think about the man on his knees. It was *his* decision, I tell myself. And besides, I'm negative. Or was, anyway, last time I checked.

This passage suggests what was happening all over Fire Island while Morgan and Ryan kissed by the pool in "Petunias." It's explicit in a straightforward, unambiguous, journalistic style: nothing is left to the imagination, neither the physical details nor the character's thoughts. It describes a culture where people play

Russian roulette every night, where sex and death compete for center stage. Here, in this passage, sex wins—though by the time Jeff goes home for the night, he well knows that death might prevail.

THE STRAIGHT COMMUNITY

In 1996, while I was promoting the first edition of *Joy,* a woman asked me how it was possible to write without awkwardness about a couple—by which she meant a straight couple—on the verge of sex who must have "the talk" before getting down to business. The answer then was that "the talk" itself is awkward—the way stopping for birth control devices can disrupt the romantic mood—and the awkwardness can be integrated into the sex scene, as Peter Carey does so delicately in the example below, published in the first edition. The answer now, in 2001, is that "the talk" is much less awkward, because we are used to it; we ourselves are less self-conscious about it, because we know that AIDS is here to stay.

This change in attitude has crept into straight-sex fiction, whether the characters are college students or well-to-do, middle-aged married people committing a bit of harmless adultery with a former spouse.

When student and teacher fall into bed together in Francine Prose's *Blue Angel,* the characters don't say a word about AIDS or condoms. The young woman deftly reaches into the night table for the little foil packet, which is so unfamiliar to the married older man that for a moment he thinks it's a tea bag. "That's sex in the nineties," he thinks, "and a good thing for them both that Angela's careful. Not that she has much to worry about from Swenson. But who knows what *she's* been up to?" He then wonders if the condom will make him lose his erection; and recalls his own early days as the member of the couple with the condom nearby. "Isn't this how girls used to feel when Swenson was in high school, and, in the midst of the spontaneous passionate necking, their boyfriend turned out to have brought along a cooly premeditated rubber?"

Prose integrates the condom and all it means—past and future—into Angela's action plucking it from the drawer and Swenson's far-reaching, unspoken thoughts.

In Alexandra Marshall's *Something Borrowed,* an ex-husband and ex-wife, each married again, end up in a hotel bed together at the weekend-long wedding of one of their children. They have what can be described as a chatty yet probing exchange about how safe the sex is that they are about to have. He doesn't have a condom; neither does she. But with a bit of direct questioning, they learn that neither has strayed from their respective marriage beds, and everyone was quite careful before that. Still, "Gail would be required to trust him as she once had." Even in this starchy, upper-middle-class, mostly monogamous community, "the talk" has become a routine part of foreplay.

AIDS, though, is not a distant fear for Ava Johnson, the narrator of *What Looks Like Crazy on an Ordinary Day* by Pearl Cleage, published in 1997. Since discovering Charlotte Watson Sherman's *The Touch* when I wrote the first edition, this is the only other novel I have found about an H.I.V.-infected woman, in this case, an African American who learned of her condition while running her own beauty salon in Atlanta. It was selected for Oprah's Book Club and became a national best-seller, putting H.I.V.-positive women on the nation's popular radar screen in a way that they had not been before.

The book is political—taking on the hypocrisy and small-mindedness of the Baptist Church—and funny; not exactly what one expects from the subject. When she learns she is infected, Ava does not know who passed on the virus to her. She writes letters to all the men she has slept with in recent years to inform them; one letter proves to be her undoing. An angry wife intercepts it, appears at Ava's beauty salon, and blares to all that Ava has AIDS. Business drops off. Ava sells the shop for a tidy sum and decides to move to San Francisco, where the H.I.V. climate is more open-minded. She stops on her way across the country to visit her sister in a small Michigan town, and ends up falling in love with her sister's neighbor, Eddie—a man with his own troubled past—and helping her sister educate local young women, many of them teenage mothers, about safe sex, money, and the rest of life, at meetings they hold in the nearby Baptist church.

To one meeting, Ava and her sister bring pamphlets about AIDS, a package of hot dogs, and condoms and conduct a demonstration, urging the young women to practice. The pious preacher's wife walks in, sweeps everything off the table, and screams, "'This is the very last time you will have a chance to desecrate the house of God with such evil.'" From then on, meetings are held in the sister's house, with record attendance.

In the meantime, Ava is becoming close to the gentle neighbor Eddie, who grows vegetables, eats well, and practices tai chi. The night after he confesses to her that he was in jail for ten years, after killing two people in a drug-induced state, she decides she can tell him her own secret. It's a lovely, tender scene, and hard-won for Ava. Though there is a great deal of high-spirited humor in this novel, we know she has lost and endured a lot to get to this moment.

Once she finally gets up the courage to say she is H.I.V.-positive, he surprises her by kissing her palm and saying, "'So that means we have to use a condom, right?'"

> He made it sound like the simplest thing in the world. I was so relieved, I wanted to fall into his arms and ask him if he would please kiss my palm like that for about three days, but we had to finish talking business first. I took a deep breath and tried to remain calm.
>
> I told him *yes*, we always had to use a condom and there was some other stuff, too. The speech they give you at those *Living with AIDS* workshops came back strong and I started reciting the rules like it was the first day of safe-sex summer camp. . . .
>
> "How about instead of telling me what I *can't* do, you tell me what I *can* do and I'll concentrate on that . . . I won't go

anywhere you don't invite me . . . Can I touch your face? . . . Can I touch your eyes? . . . Can I touch your mouth? . . . Can we take our clothes off? . . . Can I touch your breasts? . . ."

And he stroked and soothed and tickled and teased and looked and lingered and sighed and savored like he'd been waiting for this moment as long as I had. And when he saw that was bringing me to the edge of someplace I truly wanted to be, he leaned over and asked me in the sweetest possible way if he could go with me, so I took him in my hands.

This is a wonderful example of a sex scene that matters, that comes naturally from the circumstances of both characters and that is woven tightly into the fabric of the book. It's important in the scene for the narrator to be specific about physical details because there are so many rules to abide by, and both characters want to abide by them. The scene is slow and leisurely; the narrator takes pains to make the reader experience the pleasure both characters feel, despite the limitations that safe sex imposes on them.

Reading this scene, we forget—at least momentarily—to ask the question that used to be so central to our anxiety about safe sex: "How can you enjoy it when there are so many rules?" *Here's how,* Pearl Cleage declares, and for better or worse, in sorrow and joy, fear and hope, this is where we are in 2001; and where we're likely to be for quite some time.

By contrast, the tone of the AIDS chapter I wrote in 1995 has a sense of both fresh grief and quiet mournfulness that more accurately reflected the fiction being written. I called the chapter "The End of Bravado," and included these lines from Susan Sontag's short story "The Way We Live Now": "He never mentioned the prospect that even if he didn't die . . . that whatever happened it was over, the way he had lived until now . . . the end of bravado, the end of folly, the end of trusting life."

THE END OF BRAVADO (1995)

A fiction editor at a national magazine reports with some dismay that she is seeing an abundance of short story submissions in which plots turn on couples, exclusively heterosexual, deciding not to have sex because they don't have a condom and ending their evenings together with harsh words and recriminations over the matter. The rubber used as an artifice to end a date rings false to the editor; so do all the women characters who cross her desk who do not carry their own condoms, as many do in real life. By contrast, the editor notes that in stories about gay men, the absence of a condom is not enough to ruffle anyone's feathers or cut short a date. In a community decimated by AIDS, safe sex is de rigueur, and creative solutions to lust essential.

What does all this mean when it comes to devising a few general principles on writing about sex in the age of AIDS? To begin with, it means that how you and your characters approach sex *and* safe sex depends very much on your relationship to the disease. Gay characters, and the primarily gay writers who create them, live in an environment in many ways defined by the ravages and repercussions of AIDS. Illness and death have an inescapable immediacy and weight for the infected and uninfected alike; fictional characters, like their real-life counterparts, often exist in extremis, forced at every turn to explore the fusion of love, sex, mortality, and grief.

To most of the straight characters in fiction published up to now, when AIDS appears at all, it has been a much more distant threat, something that doesn't much cross their minds except when they are contemplating sex with a new partner. The act of practicing safe sex—or talking about practicing it—is often the most tangible connection to the disease these characters have.

The AIDS-aware fiction I have read leads me to conclude it could be useful to writers to organize this chapter around the differences between these two cultures as they have emerged to date in fiction. Of course, these characteristics and the fiction that explore them may well change in years to come.

A minute subgroup of fictional characters to emerge so far are heterosexual adults infected with H.I.V. or AIDS. Though AIDS-infected children have made appearances (in Alice Hoffman's *At Risk*, and a recent first novel, *Rocking the Babies*, by Linda Raymond), my research turned up only one short story, "Pandora's Box," by Janice Eidus (in the 1991 *O. Henry Prize Short Story Collection*) and one novel, *The Touch*, by Charlotte Watson Sherman (published by HarperCollins, 1995), with heterosexual, H.I.V.-positive adults, in both cases women, one of whom is sexually active.

Before examining the demands of writing about sex and safe sex in both categories, it's important to note that because we can track the emergence of AIDS and our awareness of it so precisely, the year in which you set a work of fiction is crucial to whether and how the issue of AIDS will be incorporated into your characters' behavior and attitudes. The cut-off dates will vary between gays and straights, and break down even further by the country or even city in which you set a work of fiction. Alan Hollinghurst tells us in *The Swimming-Pool Library* that his narrator is writing about the summer of 1983 in England, "the last summer of its kind there was ever to be." AIDS is never mentioned, but our certain knowledge of what is to come infuses his sex scenes with the possibility of extinction and with an added poignancy. Like today's readers of Christopher Isherwood's *Berlin Stories*, based on his experiences living in Berlin from 1929 to 1933 and published in 1939, we know something about what is to come that the characters, and in Isherwood's case the author, do not.

THE GAY COMMUNITY

AIDS has been chronicled so powerfully in fiction by writers from Reynolds Price and Edmund White to Allan Barnett and

Christopher Coe, two of many gifted young writers who have died of AIDS, that I come to the task of giving any writerly advice on the subject tugging my forelock. My hunch is that gay writers need less guidance than others in certain aspects of writing about sex these days because they possess an abundance of charged material: an enforced code of sexual behavior in which desire and grief have become permanently linked. Under these circumstances, it is not difficult to apply the principle of making a sex scene matter to your characters and the larger concerns of your story. It matters unrelentingly. As it does for the protagonist in Edmund White's story "Running on Empty": "These days, of course, desire entailed hopelessness—he'd learned to match every pant of longing with a sigh of regret."

As you study the examples in this chapter from recent fiction, consider the following observations and guidelines—in addition to the basic principles of good writing about sex described in chapters 2 and 3, which apply here as well:

1. Practicing safe sex seems to be taken for granted among gay male characters. Little conflict erupts between them around this issue except in the case of the occasional daredevil who wants to have unprotected sex. Because the norm of safe sex has been so firmly established, when a character rejects it, we should have some idea what is motivating him. Occasionally, notably in a story called "Succor" by Allan Barnett, characters negotiate beforehand what constitutes safe sex.

2. As in all sex scenes, if you go into the physical details, whether or not they refer specifically to elements of safe sex, the details should enhance the story in some way: by helping create dramatic tension and/or revealing something about the relationship, the culture, and the characters.

3. As in all good fiction involving sex, if you create the world beyond the bedroom with sufficient depth and texture, you will have more to work with when your characters seek each other out behind closed doors. This is particularly so in a setting as freighted and overdetermined as this one.

4. In quite a bit of gay fiction, sex scenes include explicit references to illness or death, but it is certainly not necessary to be explicit in order to convey the ways in which they bear down upon your characters' sexual selves.

As I look over the following excerpts from two recent short stories, I see that what unites them is a meticulous degree of attention to character as well as an awareness of AIDS so present elsewhere that it does not necessarily need to be explained in the sex scene. Each character's role in the scene flows from everything about him that has come before, creating a sense of inevitability that distinguishes the best fiction.

Grief, lust, sexual terror, and a self-mocking search for innocence are at the heart of Wesley Gibson's whimsically devastating story "Out There." Billy, the guarded, ironic protagonist who makes decorative furniture designed *not* to last, has watched his attitudes change in recent years from "cheerful pessimism to this, whatever it was," because of his proximity to so much death. After breaking up with his latest lover in a pancake house, he now wants to "date," by which he means, as he explains to his friend Clare, "real dates with going to the movies and kisses goodnight and no sex." On a date with a man he calls John Day:

> They didn't make it to the movies. Billy tried: "I don't think we should sleep together on the first date," feeling like Linda Lovelace disguised as Sandra Dee. John Day was not put off by Billy's disguise. He'd said, "Why not?" smiling and pulling Billy gently toward him by the collar. John Day had a sly, giddy smile that had disarmed Sandra Dees from time immemorial. He kissed warm and tough. He'd tested negative. It was goodbye Troy Donahue and volleyball on the beach. It was hello Deep Throat. It was hello darkness.
> They kept losing their erections.

The sense of growing sexual abandon that the author creates in the long paragraph, with Billy resisting at first and then tumbling to John's advances, is a nice setup for the punch line, which is that they are both too frightened to go through with it, even *with* safe sex. If sex was once a fleeting respite for lovers to forget their troubles for a short while, for gay men in these times it has become instead a chilling reminder of loss and potential loss.

When Billy and John meet again, "They also couldn't come. After an hour or so, they subsided into caresses, Billy rubbing little circles on John Day's belly, John Day kneading the back of Billy's neck." In the meantime, Billy has also begun dating another John ("John Two") who, he learns in short order, has tested positive. When John asks him, " 'Does it matter?' " Billy answers no. "He could have been lying. He didn't know." It leads Billy to these thoughts:

> Love. Even as a joke, it kicked up a dust of confusion. There was a time when Billy could have said, "This is love. This is grief. Here's one of me having fun." But now all his loves were streaked with grief; and all his griefs shot through with a terrible love. This borderless place he'd been shoved into was identical to the place before, but the old maps were useless, the language was subtly different; and he stumbled over the future tense of its verbs.

In a startling passage from "The *Times* As It Knows Us," by the late Allan Barnett, about a group of gay friends recently portrayed, inaccurately, they feel, in the *New York Times,* the narrator recalls his beloved lover, Samuel, who died of AIDS, and wonders how he and others can mourn their multitudinous losses. "Our condolences are arid as leaves," he thinks. "We are actors who have overrehearsed our lines." He remembers a friend urging him not to attend the funeral of a man he did not know well, but he knew it would have been perilous to deny his own grief. In order to survive, he realizes he must

> give sorrow occasion and let it go, or your heart will imprison you in constant February, a chain-link fence around frozen soil,

where your dead will stack in towers past the point of grieving. *Let your tears fall for the dead, and as one who is suffering begin the lament . . . do not neglect his burial.* Think of him, the one you loved, on his knees, on his elbows, his face turned up to look back in yours, his mouth dark in his dark beard. He was smiling because of you. You tied a silky rope around his wrists, then down around the base of his cock and balls, his anus raised for you. When you put your mouth against it, you ceased to exist. All else fell away. You had brought him, and he you, to that point where you are most your mind and most your body. His prostate pulsed against your fingers like a heart in a cave, *mind, body, body, mind,* over and over. Looking down at him, he who is dead and gone, then lying across the broken bridge of his spine, the beachhead of his back, you would gladly change places with him. *Let your weeping be bitter and your wailing fervent; then be comforted for your sorrow.* Find in grief the abandon you used to find in love; grieve the way you used to fuck.

In the way that AIDS has forced many to reinvent sexuality, this passage presents the possibility for a new literary form to accommodate the horror of AIDS: a sex scene that is part elegy, part safe sex, part prayer for the dead, and concludes with some raw, practical, self-help-style advice on learning to live with grief.

THE STRAIGHT WORLD

In my conversations with writers about this chapter, many heterosexuals have said they are stumped about how to handle safe sex in their writing, sex being the only brush with the threat of AIDS in most of their characters' lives. What I think they want to know is how to overcome the awkwardness, the inelegance, the unspontaneousness of safe sex and not call so much attention to the condom, the logistics, and the seriousness of the threat that everyone involved ceases to have a good time.

Though in real life some teenagers and adults practice safe sex with new partners, it is not the essential gesture it is in the gay community. Thus it seems, in real life and in fiction, that every encounter with a new partner is a potential wrangle over who requires safe sex, who doesn't, and exactly what it is. In Charlotte Watson Sherman's *The Touch*, her protagonist, Rayna, an African-American painter in her thirties, has what she calls "The Talk" with each new lover: she says she won't make love unless he wears a condom. When a recent suitor "fails" the talk—refuses to wear one—Rayna walks away. But with her new man, perhaps smarting from her last rejection, "she couldn't bring herself to say the words." They don't spring to his lips, either.

This issue, of learning to write about AIDS and the threat of AIDS in a largely uninfected community, is very much a work in progress. For the time being, I offer these guidelines as a place to begin:

1. If you are not on the sexual front lines these days, do some research: talk to people who are. Ask them what takes place in their intimate exchanges around this issue. Obviously, there is no one scenario, but getting a sense of the atmosphere and possibilities may help you create the right scenario for your characters, in keeping with who they are.

2. Whether or not you do research, explore your own reactions to this issue and *use those feelings* in developing your characters' actions and reactions. If, for example, you feel awkward, self-conscious, and preoccupied with regret that sex has come to this, remember: your characters might feel that way, too.

3. Don't be politically correct and artistically feeble. It's not enough for your characters to carry condoms and take them out at the appropriate moment. Use the device and the issue to enrich the work, to bring us closer to the characters and the moment.

4. If you are writing about characters who are infected, feelings of fear, illness, and loss may be more immediate.

5. If writing about safe sex seems as confining as having it may, surprise us—and yourself—and have some fun with it, as Australian writer Peter Carey does in this passage from his novel *The Tax Inspector.* Toward the end of the novel, an unlikely union has developed between Maria Takis and Jack Catchprice. She's a left-leaning tax inspector, eight months pregnant and no longer seeing the married man who fathered her child. Jack, a slick, successful real estate developer, is kin to (though not in business with) the crazy, eccentric Catchprice family, who own a failing car dealership whose illegal accounting methods have come to the attention of the tax inspector. In Jack's bed late at night, Maria is self-conscious about her body and reluctant to sleep with someone whose values are so alien to her own. She professes to be too pregnant to concentrate on his seduction. He answers:

"We could try. We could just lie here."

"I don't know you. . . . It's not smart for people to just jump into bed anymore."

"Is this a discussion about the Unmentionable?"

"I don't want to offend you."

"You don't offend me at all. We could play it safe."

"*Safer,* not actually safe," she smiled. While still involved in her monogamous adulterous relationship with Alistair, she had complacently pitied those who must go through this. She had never thought that the tone of the conversation might be quite so tender.

He touched her on the forehead between her eyes and ran his finger down the line of her nose. "I'll make love to you 100 percent safe."

She had never imagined you could say those words and still feel tender, but now she was lying on her side and he was lying on his and he had those clear blue Catchprice eyes and such sweet crease marks around his eyes. . . .

"Is there 100 percent?" she asked.

"Is this safe?"

"Hmm?"

"Does this feel safe?"

"Jack, don't."

"Don't worry. I'll keep my word. Is this safe?"

"Of course."

She let him undress her and caress her swollen body. God, she thought—this is how people die.

"Is this beautiful to you?"

"Oh yes," he said. "You glisten. . . ."

She began to kiss him, to kiss his chest, to nuzzle her face among the soft apple-sweet hairs, discovering as she did so a hunger for the scents and textures of male skin.

"Get the condom," she heard herself say.

"You sure?"

"Mmm."

"I've got it."

"I'm crazy," she said.

The passage, one of the few extended fictional exchanges involving heterosexual safe sex, and by far the most interesting, uses Maria's embarrassment, awkwardness, and fear to create the dramatic conflict that drives the scene. The exchange is full of surprises. My favorite is Maria's final "yes," which manages to rewrite for the age of AIDS Molly Bloom's great announcement of openness to sexual passion in James Joyce's *Ulysses*—"yes I said yes I will yes"—to this: "'Get the condom.'"

The abundance of dialogue creates an intimacy and immediacy that draws us right into bed with Maria and Jack. They surprise each other and the reader with their mix of nervousness (Maria's), suaveness (Jack's), collective good humor, and tenderness. Safe sex is both serious and playful in a way that accurately reflects the degree of danger these characters feel.

How fiction writers of the future will incorporate H.I.V. and AIDS into their characters' sex lives will depend very much on what course the disease takes in real life. For the time being, recent literature suggests that those venturing into this territory have a few more choices than they might have imagined.

The remainder of this book will concentrate on techniques for writing about sex, as well as strategies for reading, that focus on the relationship between sexual partners. I begin each chapter with a discussion of what characterizes the relationship and what these characteristics mean to a fiction writer—what possibilities they offer us. Next, I list some "Given Circumstances," what I think of as general truths about such a relationship that should be incorporated into our sex scenes. Not every given circumstance will be true in every case, but many will be. Following the list are examples of writing meant to illustrate particular points and provide a range of the possibilities for combining the general with the specific.

While I separate the issue of writing about sex in the age of AIDS from writing about types of relationships, the guidelines I offer here are meant to supplement those that follow.

5

Losing Your Cherry and Other First Times to Remember

> Leota was bold. She wasn't afraid to touch anything and
> where her knowledge came from was a secret but she knew
> what she was after. And I soon found out.
>
> — RITA MAE BROWN,
> *Rubyfruit Jungle*

Losing your virginity has more in common with getting a driver's
license than we like to think. The plastic-sealed card that fits in
your wallet doesn't mean you know all you need to know about
driving; it means you've been given permission to find out first-
hand everything you don't know.

First-time lovers, even if they have the legitimacy of a marriage
license, are usually young, nervous, and doing the deed in either
unfamiliar or uncomfortable surroundings: the bridal suite, the
backseat of a car, the teenager's narrow twin bed, or the prostitute's chamber. (Wedding nights and honeymoons are so special,
I've devoted the next chapter to them.) Put another way, no one's

first time is likely to be a sexual tsunami. It's not supposed to be; it's just supposed to push you through the starting gate and get you going. It may be over not long after it begins. For women it may be extremely painful. Or it may be so unsatisfactory that it leaves one or both partners scratching their heads and wondering if they misread the directions, as a pair of newlyweds does in Joseph Heller's satiric novel about World War II, *Catch-22*, until Doc Daneeka shows them, with the aid of rubber models in his office, what goes where.

What does all this mean for the fiction writer? It means you don't have to worry about writing a sex scene so hot you'd be embarrassed to show it to your mother, who, don't forget, had a first time herself. It means there are some interesting possibilities for conflict and drama between the lovers involving one's experience versus the other's innocence; one's timidity against the other's temerity; her nonchalance bumping up against his fear. It means your characters will be in a heightened state of awareness—accentuating feelings of awkwardness and self-consciousness—because, after all, this is a once-in-a-lifetime thing. This is a Big Deal. This is the jackknife off the high diving board. But, of course, it's almost always a disappointment, until you get the hang of it.

Because first times are so much about new physical sensations, your fictional characters are likely to be paying a lot of attention to their genitals, not because they are powerhouses of pleasure, but because we know they are supposed to be, and we want to be sure to be paying attention in case the transformation happens. It's like a child in a car asking "Are we there yet?" During your first time, particularly if you're female, it's difficult to know whether you're there yet.

We only ever get one First Time, but there can be more than one *kind* of first time: the technical initiation versus what I call "The First Time That Matters" or "The First Time I Understood Why This Is Such a Big Deal," which may occur years later. I've included here a second chance at the first time from a short story by Edmund White, as well as another White example of a beautifully rendered moment in a gay teenage boy's life from *A Boy's Own Story.*

For middle-aged lovers, there is also an erotically knowing category of first times that a passage from Mary Gordon's novel *Spending* captures. In a different vein, a scene from A. M. Homes's satiric novel *Music For Torching* involves two suburban housewives having a first time on the kitchen floor.

For young people learning about sex and love in America these days, it is difficult to convey how much a woman's—though not a man's—virginity used to mean, and how many classic works of fiction, from Samuel Richardson's eighteenth-century epistolary novel *Clarissa,* to Thomas Hardy's nineteenth-century *Tess of the D'Urbervilles* (subtitled *A Pure Woman*), turn on the loss or threatened loss of female virtue, synonymous back then with virginity. "The debauching of a virgin may be her ruin and make her for life unhappy," said Benjamin Franklin in his essay "Advice on the Choice of a Mistress." The injustice of the double standard was not lost on the early-twentieth-century anarchist Emma Goldman in her essay "The Traffic in Women":

> Society considers the sex experiences of a man as attributes of his general development, while similar experiences in the life of a woman are looked upon as a terrible calamity, a loss of honor and of all that is good and noble in a human being.

In her celebrated novel *The Group,* Mary McCarthy, who wrote scorchingly about women's sex lives long before birth control pills were a gleam in anyone's eye, presented a group of Vassar graduates in the 1930s. Their ideas about sex were shaped by both the boldness of the Roaring Twenties and the ignorance of the Victorian era, when British wives were advised to "grip the bed and think of

England" to endure their marital duties. In a scene from *The Group* too long to be included here, Dottie Renfrew, known as "Boston," class of '33, is eager to lose her virginity to the best man at her classmate's wedding, Dick Brown, who she thought "was so frightfully attractive and unhappy and had so much to give."

When I was twelve years old, this scene was passed around as the smut of our day, and particularly the passage after Dick deflowers Dottie, examines the sheet beneath her, and says, referring to another girlfriend, this one quite unlucky, " 'Betty bled like a pig.' " I knew that sex had occurred, but knew nothing of hymens and their properties, and read this line at least 600 times, my brow permanently wrinkled in bemusement. When I read the scene again recently, Betty bleeding like a pig was of no consequence compared to the wicked dialogue and McCarthy's wry feminist leanings. Dottie is so naive she has no idea how badly Dick is treating her and no idea she has had an orgasm until he tells her. Even then she is not convinced:

> "You *came*, Boston," he remarked. . . . "I mean you had an orgasm." Dottie made a vague, still inquiring noise in her throat; she was pretty sure, now, she understood, but the new word discombobulated her. "A climax," he added, more sharply. "Do they teach you that word at Vassar?" . . . "It's normal then?" she wanted to know, beginning to feel better. Dick shrugged. "Not for girls of your upbringing. Not the first time, usually. Appearances to the contrary, you're probably highly sexed."

Reading this scene again, all I can think is, dirty books are wasted on the young.

GIVEN CIRCUMSTANCES

1. Particularly when it's a woman's first time with a man, it's almost certain sex will *not* be of the sizzling, earth-moving

variety. For the woman it may feel more like a surgical proce-
dure without anesthesia.
2. The first time is a major rite of passage. People often have
   great expectations for it and devote a good bit of time afterward wondering if the actuality met their expectations—the
   Before and After exercise. Because of these expectations,
   people are in a heightened state of awareness.
3. It's likely the characters don't know each other well.
4. One or both may be young, timid, anxious, ignorant, and/or
   fearful, afraid of the unknown, of pregnancy, disease, or
   being caught.
5. The setting often is not a place of one's own.
6. Customs and expectations about the first time vary with age,
   gender, religion, and cultural background.
7. For gays and lesbians and others for whom sex is forbidden,
   the first time may have complex elements of anxiety, guilt,
   shame, rebellion, relief, and/or liberation.

EXAMPLES

With any luck, it begins with a kiss.

There is no one who writes better about physical sensations—
not limited to the sexual—than Jamaica Kincaid, and no first
kisses in recent literature as memorable as those described in her
1990 coming-of-age novel, *Lucy*, in a chapter called, appropriately, "The Tongue."

As with all of Kincaid's work, the story proceeds as an intricate
series of memories, with thoughts of one event triggering a deep
childhood memory, which then triggers another and eventually
returns to the present story. But the real story is always the narrator's phenomenal intelligence and capacity to make these shim-
mering connections.

It doesn't do the writing justice to quote brief passages, but I
think a taste of her work will lead readers to the books themselves.

At fourteen I had discovered that a tongue had no real taste. I was sucking the tongue of a boy named Tanner, and I was sucking his tongue because I liked the way his fingers looked on the keys of the piano as he played it, and I had liked the way he looked from the back as he walked across the pasture, and also, when I was close to him, I liked the way behind his ears smelled. Those three things had led to my standing in his sister's room (she was my best friend), my back pressed against the closed door, sucking his tongue. Someone should have told me that there were other things to seek out in a tongue than the flavor of it, for then I would not have been standing there sucking on poor Tanner's tongue as if it were an old Frozen Joy with all its flavor run out and nothing left but the ice. As I was sucking away, I was thinking, Taste is not the thing to seek out in a tongue; how it makes you feel—that is the thing. I used to like to eat boiled cow's tongue served in a sauce of lemon juice, onions, cucumbers, and pepper; but cow's tongue has no real taste either. It was the sauce that made the cow's tongue so delicious to eat.

This passage, like many of Kincaid's, has a deceptive simplicity. There is no memory or sensation too inconsequential to escape her notice. Most of the words have one syllable; the ideas are straightforward and unadorned: *I liked the way behind his ears smelled.* . . . *I used to eat boiled cow's tongue.* . . . The power of the writing is in the tension between the simplicity of the language and the intensity and focus on how the girl experiences and understands the kisses physically and intellectually. She is remembering back to a time of innocence, when she did not know what she knows now, *and* she is scrupulous about telling us how it felt then.

In her 1989 coming-of-age novel, *The Floating World,* Cynthia Kadohata describes narrator Olivia's first time with a boyfriend named Tan, who works with her at a chicken hatchery in

Arkansas. They are both sixteen and have been necking and petting in an abandoned bus in the hatchery yard, thrilled by the possibility of being caught. Olivia is illegitimate, and she has grown up acutely conscious of the sexual arrangements and feelings of her mother and stepfather, her grandmother, and other adults, so that she is open to her own sexuality.

When Olivia and Tan plan quite matter-of-factly to make love, they go to his parents' empty house, intending to use their bed. What Olivia has been reading recently in her grandmother's diaries is on her mind and part of her motivation to make love. In addition to her three husbands, Grandmother had seven lovers. About one of them she wrote that when they argued, she felt strong. Olivia realizes that more than wanting to feel love, she wants to feel the same strength her grandmother felt in the presence of a man.

Olivia and Tan end up in Tan's bed, kissing under the covers. Before long, Olivia panics about soiling the sheets and insists they move to the bathroom floor. Reluctantly, Tan agrees, but once they get there and she lies down on the cold, hard tiles, she wants to go back to the bed:

"Let's just stay," he said, breathing hard.

"Well, okay." I closed my eyes as tightly as I could. "I'm ready," I said bravely. When nothing happened, I opened my eyes.

He looked at me as if he had amnesia. Then he looked surprised, then frustrated. "Okay, okay," he said, half pulling me up. We stood and I saw his erection and was so surprised I walked into the doorjamb on the way out. When we got in bed I was surprised how ready I was, and how easily he slipped in. He moved in and out hard at first, making my head hit against the headboard. I wouldn't have minded, except I was scared I might get knocked out, and then I'd miss the most important part; but that didn't happen.

I expected that afterward I would feel some emotion related to love, and I did, but I also had a peculiar feeling a shade shy of self-confidence.

When first-time lovers are young and living at home, the question of *where* to do the deed is all important. Kadohata exploits this element and makes the actual place a source of humor and conflict between Olivia and Tan.

Both Olivia's nervousness and her enthusiasm are essential to the appeal of the scene. Let's look at how both work:

Olivia's nervous need to keep moving creates action and conflict. Had Olivia and Tan kept kissing under the covers with one predictable thing leading to the another, we would have had a much less lively scene. Kadohata makes Olivia so nervous that she insists on playing musical beds and floors. Her boyfriend, much more aroused than she is and less concerned about leaving evidence, challenges her but gives in every time. This gentle, innocent tension between them gives the scene an element of conflict. It also reveals Olivia's nervousness through her actions rather than through direct statements about her state of mind.

Olivia's nervousness is a counterpoint to her enthusiasm. Olivia's plucky openness to the experience makes a nice contrast to her jangling nerves. Had Kadohata dwelled on the nervousness without injecting so much of Olivia's enthusiasm, the scene would have been flatter. Ironically, Olivia thinks she is motivated to make love by wanting some of her grandmother's strength, but as we see in this scene, she already has plenty of self-confidence and a clear idea of what she wants.

Molly Bolt, the tough, feisty narrator of Rita Mae Brown's *Rubyfruit Jungle,* published in 1973, did for lesbian rights what *Fear of Flying* would do a year later for the female orgasm. In sixth grade, Molly proposes marriage to a girl called Leota, whose own plans for her life at that point turn out to be remarkably prescient: "'I'll get married and have six children and wear an apron like my mother, only my husband will be handsome.'" In the meantime, Leota is very keen on kissing Molly, and more. During a sleepover date, they finish watching Milton Berle on television, shut the bedroom door, kiss for hours, and take off their pajamas:

> It was much better without the pajamas. I could feel her cool skin all over my body. That really was a lot better. Leota started kissing me with her mouth open. Now my stomach was going to fall out on the floor. . . . We kept on. . . . She began to touch me all over and I knew I was really going to die. Leota was bold. She wasn't afraid to touch anything and where her knowledge came from was a secret, but she knew what she was after. And I soon found out.
>
> The next morning we went to school like any two sixth-grade girls.

Molly's wide-eyed openness to these events is in keeping with her already advanced sexual adventures: until she was caught, she ran a nickel-a-look business venture, parading the uncircumcised penis of her friend Broccoli. But this night with Leota isn't business; it's her first sexual experience as a girl who will grow up to love women.

Soon after that first night, Molly's family moves away and the friends are separated until 1968 when Molly, now a student of filmmaking at NYU and what she calls a "devil-may-care lesbian," visits Leota in their hometown. Leota is married, has two kids, and at twenty-four looks forty-five. When Molly asks if she ever thinks of that night, Leota says,

> "I'm too busy for that stuff. Who has time to think? Anyway, that was perverted, sick. I haven't got time for it. . . . Why did you ask me that? Why'd you come back here—to ask me that?

You must have stayed that way. Is that why you're walking around in jeans and a pullover? You one of those sickies? . . . A pretty girl like you. You could have lots of men. You have more choices than I did here in this place."

When characters who have a same-sex first time in childhood meet again in adulthood and one or both have grown up to be gay, the early scene can take on a significance it might not have had for the characters at that time.

Alternatively, for gay characters or children with homosexual feelings, a same-sex first time can be a major event in which characters feel not only sexually satisfied but relieved and liberated from the tyranny of trying to conform to a sexuality that doesn't fit.

For the fourteen-year-old boy called Ed in Edmund White's story "Reprise," there are two distinct categories of first times—the technical first time and the first time that matters. "Until now," he tells us, "the people I'd had sex with were boys at camp who pretended to hypnotize each other or married men who cruised the Howard Street Elevated toilets and drove me down to the beach in station wagons filled with their children's toys."

But when, in 1954, Ed falls for Jim Grady, the college-age son of the man his mother is dating, he experiences the generous sex and affection of a man less inclined to lead a double life. The two boys connive to spend the night together at Ed's house, after watching *The Perry Como Show* with Ed's mother. Jim feigns drunkenness and insists on sleeping over, rather than drive home in his condition. In Ed's room, where there is an extra bed:

He lay back with a heavy-lidded, cool expression I suspected was patterned on Como's, but I didn't care, I was even pleased he wanted to impress me as I scaled his body, felt his great warm arms around me, tasted the Luckies and the Bud on his lips. . . . "Hey," he whispered, and smiled at me as his hands cupped my twenty-six-inch waist and my hot penis planted its flag on the stony land of his perfect body. "Hey," he said, hitching me higher and deeper into his presence.

The surprise here for the reader is the significance of the single word "Hey" to the young narrator. Ironically, in this slight utterance Ed finds acceptance, intimacy, and affection, different from what he found with boys and men who hid their desires with hypnotism and family life. "Jim was the first man who took off his clothes, held me in his arms, looked me in the eye, and said, 'Hey.'" Though he does not describe his encounters with these other men, we have to assume, from the weight he gives to "Hey," that they were starkly anonymous; that his partners were so uncomfortable with what they were doing that they could not even look at him, much less offer a mild endearment. As a result of Ed and Jim's brief association, Ed's mother discovers his homosexuality. His father is told, he is sent to a psychiatrist and to boarding school: "My entire life changed."

Forty years later the two men meet in a Paris hotel room: "When he hitched me into his embrace and said, 'Hey,' I felt fourteen again." The men's bodies have broadened and withered with age, but the nostalgic repetition of this single word is a kind of aphrodisiac.

- Intimacy can be conveyed in very small packages, in words of one syllable.
- Don't be shy about letting your first-time lovers meet again in adulthood. They won't all turn out to be Leota from *Rubyfruit Jungle*.

In reading *A Boy's Own Story* recently, I came upon one of the hypnosis-at-summer-camp scenes the narrator in White's short story glancingly refers to. It's a wonderful passage about a much more childlike first time:

Where the path crossed the logger's road, Ralph was sitting in a sort of natural hammock created by the exposed roots of an old elm. He had his pants down around his knees and was examining his erect penis with a disbelieving curiosity, a slightly stunned look emptying his face. He called me over and I joined him, as though to examine a curiosity of nature. He persuaded me to touch it and I did. He asked me to lick the red, sticky, unsheathed head and I hesitated. Was it dirty? I wondered. Would someone see us? Would I become ill? Would I become a queer and never, never be like other people?

To overcome my scruples, Ralph hypnotized me. He didn't have to intone the words long to send me into a deep trance. Once I was under his spell he told me I'd obey him, and I did. He also said that when I awakened I'd remember nothing, but he was wrong there. I have remembered everything.

To me, the two most interesting aspects of the passage are that the boy tells us nothing about the physical experience about to happen; he gives it to us to imagine, with the haunting, Proustian last line. Second, I think we are meant to take with some irony the narrator's line, "He didn't have to intone the words long to send me into a deep trance." The boy *wanted* to be hypnotized because he wanted permission to proceed with some assurance that engaging in this act would not "brand" him for life.

A different sort of same-sex first time occurs in A. M. Homes's satiric novel *Music for Torching*. The first-time encounter is between two suburban housewives after their children and husbands have left in the morning. Elaine and Paul, whose house was damaged by fire, are staying with neighbors, Pat and her husband, George. The scene is long and hilarious, full of embarrassed tittering and reluctant tumbling to unfamiliar sensations. The come-on begins when Elaine splashes coffee on her white shirt and Pat, still in her bathrobe, tells her to take it off and proceeds to remove the stain—and then kiss her. Elaine's alarm and confusion about what's going on and why run through the scene, summarized in the word "fine." Pat's ease and Elaine's discomfort are the primary sources of conflict that propel the encounter and give it its energy and humor. A few highlights:

It's fine, Elaine tells herself, if it's only a kiss. Fine as long as the clothing is on, fine if only her shirt is off, fine if. . . . She's making rules and instantly breaking them.

Pat is at her breast. A noise escapes Elaine, an embarrassing deep sigh—like air rushing out of something. Elaine can't believe that she's letting this happen; she's not stopping it, she's not screaming, she's enjoying it. . . . Elaine can't tell who is who, what is what—Marcel Marceau, a mirror game, each miming the other.

A few minutes later:

And Pat is on top, grinding against Elaine, humping her in a strangely prickless pose. Fucking that's all friction. . . .
"It's fine," Elaine says. . . .
"Fine if it's only on the outside, fine if it's just a hand. Fine if it's fingers and not a tongue, and then fine if it is a tongue. . . . It's all fine."
"You're a treat," Pat says. "A delicacy. I never get to kiss. George doesn't like it."

When it's over:

"Are you all right?" Pat asks.
"It's fine," Elaine says, hurrying. . . . She is suffering the strange anxiety of having risen so far up and out of herself as to seem entirely untethered. She's scared herself—as though this

has never been done before, as though she and Pat invented it right there on the kitchen floor.

A middle-aged woman full of gratitude rather than alarm is the lover in Mary Gordon's sensual feast, *Spending*, which is subtitled "A Utopian Divertimento." A divorced painter with two children in college meets a rich man who wants to be her patron, her muse, and her lover. There's a dreamy ease and self-knowledge during their first encounter in his lavish Cape Cod summer house late one night. It's also an excellent example of how to be explicit without using any of the awkward anatomical words at our disposal:

> He put his head between my legs, nuzzling at first. His beard was a little rough on the insides of my thighs. Then with his lips, then his tongue, he struck fire. I had to cry out in aston-ishment, in gratitude at being touched in that right place. Somehow, it always makes me grateful when a man finds the right place, maybe because when I was young so many of them kept finding the wrong place, or a series of wrong places, or no place at all. That strange feeling: gratitude and hunger. My hunger was being teased. It almost felt like a punishment. I kept thinking of the word "thrum," a cross between a throb and hum. I saw a flame trying to catch; I heard it, there was something I was *after*, something I was trying to achieve, and there was always the danger that I'd miss it, I wouldn't find it, or get hold of it. The terrible moment when you're afraid you won't, you'll lose it, it won't work, you won't work, it *is* unworkable and you are very, very desperate. At the same time, you want to stay in this place of desperation . . . at the same time, you're saying to yourself, you're almost there, you're almost there, you can't possibly lose it now, keep on, keep on a bit longer, you are nearly there, I know it, don't give up, you cannot lose it. Then suddenly you're there.

SOME LAST WORDS ABOUT THE FIRST TIME

What makes a first-time sex scene successful is what makes *all* good sex scenes work. As you write and rewrite, remember:

- A sex scene is not a sex manual for beginners. Stay with your characters' internal and external struggles, not only with their physical urges.
- Set up conflicts, obstacles, and surprises for your characters that spring from who they are and their circumstances at the time.
- Integrate some or all of the given circumstances into the specific moment, or create a universe in which expectations are so different that the usual given circumstances do not apply.
- If a sex scene feels obligatory or gratuitous, leave it out or rewrite it to make it essential to the story or to our understanding of the characters.

6

GREAT EXPECTATIONS: THE
WEDDING NIGHT AND
THE HONEYMOON

You can have good sex on your honeymoon and still
suspect that there's something fishy going on.
—CHARLES BAXTER,
The Feast of Love

In the days before men and women routinely lived together
before (or instead of) marriage, the honeymoon was the official
start of a couple's sex life. In many cultures and tradition-bound
religions, the honeymoon is still a rite of passage that can involve
rituals, community involvement, and evidence—the bloody bed-
sheet displayed in the window.

But even if it is not the beginning of a couple's intimacy, even
when people marry who have been living together for years, the
wedding night and the honeymoon retain an eerie, overwhelming
significance. It is our first turn at being married, the opening
scene in what we hope will be a long story with a happy ending.
And it's the beginning of legally sanctioned sex. As we saw in
the previous chapter, if our first sexual experience occurs outside

marriage, it occurs in private, in secret; we usually take pains to conceal the event. But with marriage license in hand, we are actually *expected* to make love and if for some reason that doesn't occur, lawyers and judges can get involved. A marriage that is never consummated can be easily annulled. A spouse's withdrawal from sexual relations is usually grounds for divorce. But even without legal intervention, a honeymoon that goes awry can cast a long, dark shadow over a marriage.

If all of this weighty expectation, this intimacy-on-demand, makes newlyweds nervous, it offers a sumptuously rich setting for fiction writers. Where there is expectation, expectation can be dashed. Where the stakes are high, even a small loss can be acutely painful. The more we want from a sexual experience, the greater our disappointment when it fails to live up to our fantasies.

With newlyweds more than with most other pairs of lovers, it's easy to imagine people's thoughts: *Have I made the right choice? Will she always love me? Will I always love him?* There are few sexual encounters more inherently fraught with anxiety than the wedding night—except of course the adulterous liaison.

GIVEN CIRCUMSTANCES

Some of the given circumstances here are identical to those in the previous chapter on first-time lovers. Consider these as well:

1. The characters' sexual histories and attitudes will play a part in how they relate. Are they virgins, old-time lovers, or does one have far more experience than the other?
2. They are both likely to feel a good deal of emotional and sexual pressure: performance anxiety, general anxiety, self-consciousness.
3. They may experience joy, wonder, excitement, and hopefulness at the newness and possibility of their circumstances.
4. Because of their change in legal status, their thoughts while making love may involve wondering specifically how the sex,

and their lives in general, are different now that they are married.

5. Their thoughts may also look ahead to the future, to imagine having children, a house, a family life similar to or different from their parents' lives.

6. The gravity of their new circumstances may cause them to be seized with doubt, fear, second thoughts, and possibly to see something troubling in their partner they had not noticed before or that their partner had not yet revealed to them.

7. A wonderful honeymoon is no guarantee of permanent bliss.

EXAMPLES

Without telling you the context, here is a summary paragraph—which ends a chapter—about Paula and Charlo Spencer's honeymoon in Irish writer Roddy Doyle's celebrated 1996 novel, *The Woman Who Walked Into Doors*. Paula is narrating, looking back almost twenty years to their week at a bed and breakfast owned by a Mrs. Doyle:

I couldn't get enough of him. I was tired and sore but I didn't care. I didn't want to sleep. I wanted the ache. I wanted him in me, all the time. His weight on top of me. I wanted to squeeze him in further and further. I wanted to watch his face. I wanted his sweat to drop onto me. I wanted to drop mine on him. I got on top of him. I'd never done it before. I couldn't really believe it; I was doing this. I was inventing something. I held him and put him in. He felt deeper in me. I'll never forget it. I was in charge and he liked it. I held his hands down. He pretended he was trying to break free. I let my tits touch his face. He went mad; he bucked. He split me in two. I pushed down. I couldn't believe it. One of his fingers flicked over my bum. I did it to him. He lifted and heaved. I couldn't believe it. There was no end to it, no end to the new things. He did something. I copied him. I did something. He did it back. He took me from behind. I pushed back, forced more of him into me. I sucked him. He licked me. I made him come on my stomach. He sucked my toes. The whole room rocked and Mrs. Doyle smiled at us every morning.

Out of context, the passage is a piece of pure joy; seclusion and days of uninhibited sex, with the B&B owner's blessing. But the passage comes on page 152 of the novel, long after we know that its innocence and joy are a distant memory. After four children and eighteen years of Charlo's cruelty, Paula kicked him out. A year later a policeman came to her door to report that he was dead, shot by police after he killed a woman he had taken hostage.

The novel opens with Paula remembering the officer at her door. From there she remembers the anguished days that followed, interspersed with the years that led up to them: her happy Dublin childhood, her courtship with Charlo, their wedding, their honeymoon. She's trying to figure out what happened to her happiness, her marriage, her self.

Her vivid recollection of the honeymoon is a turning point for Paula—and for the novel. The act of remembering, almost reexperiencing the openness of the sex, opens Paula up enough so that in the chapter immediately after the honeymoon passage, she admits to us in detail and at length the most painful pain of her marriage: physical closeness became regular physical brutality, inflicted by her husband and condoned by society. When Charlo took his battered wife to the hospital time and again, the doctors and nurses accepted her obviously bogus explanation: she'd walked into a door. She would have gladly told them the truth, she tells us, had anyone asked her.

The honeymoon sex as Paula recalls it here is sweet, sexy, raunchy, loving—but because we read it through the filter of all the heartache that we know came after, the passage is poignantly overlaid with unstated feelings of grief, loss, and time passing.

. . .

Bradley and Diana's honeymoon in Charles Baxter's richly comic novel *The Feast of Love* is heartbreaking in a lighter register. Baxter's method—each chapter is the voice of a different character telling his or her story—allows us to collect information about these folks that they don't always reveal to each other. Case in point: Bradley, who has a dog also named Bradley—to give you a sense of his haplessness—is in love with Diana and plans to marry her. But we've learned separately from Diana that she is still involved with a married man with whom she has an intense physical relationship. She goes ahead and marries Bradley, but he senses trouble the first night. After they've made love as "man and wife, as wedded partners, instead of just lovers, Diana said, 'Bradley, you're such a nice guy,' as she drifted off to sleep. . . . I'll take my compliments where I can get them, but 'nice' is not what a man wants to hear under these particular circumstances. . . . Speechlessness will do just fine."

Several nights later, once they're ensconced at a remote inn, Diana's behavior is so alien that Bradley finally realizes what the reader has known all along:

> Up in the bedroom, between us, Diane brought more fever to our lovemaking than she ever had before, but it was the wrong fever, as if she were trying to get rid of an internal pressure through physical means. She would ride me and close her eyes, and she would bend down to kiss my eyelids, and there wouldn't be a sprig of affection in it, not a single solitary sign of love. It was just something she needed. . . . She told me we were going to skip dinner. . . . I'd fall asleep and wake up to feel her working on me. She wouldn't let me sleep. We had bruises. I never imagined this happening, but no matter how naive you sometimes think I am, I knew that whole night, by then, watching her, that she was in love with someone else, intensely, and had always been, and been tormented by it, and now she was taking it out on me, and making it obvious and those were

her thoughts, the ones she couldn't tell me, not for a penny, not for a pound.

We had some great times, Diana and me, but we couldn't last, and we didn't.

These chilling passages remind me of Edmund White's comment that sex is the "most intense dialogue that could possibly go on between two people in which you're never sure what the other person is thinking." The brilliance in the second scene is that Baxter has made Diana's sexual behavior so extreme and self-involved that she gives Bradley enough information to *divine* what she's thinking. Because Baxter has structured the book so that we've already seen Diana with her married lover, we know, when Bradley finally "reads" Diana's mind, that he's right.

Doyle's and Baxter's newlyweds have sex in a contemporary idiom, in our era of sexual freedom for men and women. In *Plains Song,* for which Wright Morris won the National Book Award in 1981, the newlyweds have their first sexual encounter at an inn while crossing the country in a covered wagon, circa 1900—and what a difference a century makes.

If the three words that we associate with the wedding night are "I love you," the three that get attached to the union of twenty-year-old Cora and Emerson Atkins are "horse bit her." The book opens as the aged Cora is bedridden and dying. Wright describes a scar on her hand "blue as gun metal between the first and second knuckle, a seam on the flesh. How did she acquire it? It is said a horse bit her. For a farmer's wife that is not unusual."

In the first chapter, we learn the bleak story of her unromantic courtship and wedding, in rural Ohio. Once married, husband and wife, who barely know each other, set off in a covered wagon for the husband's piece of homestead government land on the Great Plains. "For Cora, this trip would constitute her honeymoon, the pause between her life such as it had once been and the endless chores of a farmer's wife."

The newlyweds spend their first several nights sleeping separately, she in a spot he had prepared for her in the wagon, he on the ground beneath. "Whatever Emerson's feelings or thoughts in such matters, they were like hers in that he kept them to himself." The sleeping arrangements "seemed to her an example of the wisdom she might expect from her husband. It was not the time or place, weary and physically sore, for whatever it was she had been led to expect."

That comes a night or two later when they stay at an inn along the Mississippi River. After their meal, Cora goes to bed. Emerson bathes and comes to bed in a "suit of oatmeal-colored flannel." They do not speak, they do not touch.

> Before he puffed the lamp out and rolled toward her, the bed creaking like the body of the wagon, her dismay had given way to dread that paralyzed her will. When he moved on her, his groping hands confusing the sheet with her nightgown, she had already put her clenched fist into her mouth and stared sightlessly at the ceiling. What did she experience? It might be likened to an operation without the anesthesia. Horror exceeded horror. The time required by her assailant to do what must be done left her in shock. In the dawn light she found that she had bitten through the flesh of her hand, exposing the bone. Emerson's bafflement moved him to speech. Aloud he asked how such a thing might have happened. Unable to grasp it, he seemed to doubt what he saw.

When he takes her to a doctor and the doctor asks what happened, Emerson answers for her: "Horse bit her."

It is their first and last sexual encounter, and the night they conceive their only daughter. Though *Plains Song* goes forward to the 1970s, Morris's characters never go out of character and *talk* about their sad history—or their future; they are so ill-equipped to thrive sexually because of the worlds they came from that not even the nonverbal physicality of sex offers them a way to connect again.

Connecting sexually is not a problem for a most unusual set of newlyweds—the real-life Bunker brothers and real-life Yates sisters—who married in North Carolina in 1843. This union was the inspiration for Darin Strauss's first novel, *Chang and Eng*, a largely invented story based on what little information there is about the sad, complicated, conjoined lives of the original "Siamese" twins, born in 1811 in Siam and connected forever by a band of flesh and ligament at their chests. (There is a haunting photograph of them on the cover of the novel, hardcover and paperback.) The historic record tells us they married sisters, one of whom had disgraced herself and her family in their small southern town by sleeping with a slave. After that, no one else would have them—until the Bunker brothers came to town. Their marriages produced twenty-one children.

Most of us will not have occasion to write about the sex lives of conjoined twins, but Strauss's decision to include several sex scenes in his novel—and what he told me in our interview in chapter 1—illustrate a number of lessons worth reiterating. Strauss reported that it is known the brothers "developed a method by which the inactive brother tried to give the busier one a little privacy. Beyond that, I invented." He also stressed that he wanted the scenes to be tasteful: "I think the danger with a story like the one I chose to tell is that, in inept hands, it might easily veer toward the crass and sensationalistic. I wasn't interested in cheap voyeurism with these sex scenes, in making the book a literary variant of the freak shows that took such awful advantage of Chang and Eng while they lived."

First, the inclusion of sex scenes in *Chang and Eng* is an extreme example of using sex to tell us something fundamental about the nature of a couple's intimacy—in this case, two couples. A sex scene can and should dramatize an essential truth about who the characters are. Lovers who are awkward and uncommunicative in bed are probably the same way in the kitchen. The problems Chang, Eng, and their wives have in bed are precisely those they have when they are not in bed. True privacy does not exist for the men; true intimacy does not exist for the married couples. They are bound together in a cruel hoax of what closeness means and what marriage means. They are truly prisoners of their bodies.

Second, the sex scene has to have the same tone as the rest of the story.

Third, writing sex scenes should not be an excuse to give voice to one's sexual fantasies. As with all fiction writing, when composing and rewriting, the writer should be trying to inhabit the body and mind of his characters. Who the characters are and what they want from a sex scene should propel the writing, not the writer's own erotic musings.

More so than with other novels, the "first" honeymoon scene in *Chang and Eng* is difficult to appreciate fully out of context. (The brothers decided that all their sexual encounters would be threesomes, rather than foursomes, so there are two separate first times.) They're too long to include here in their entirety, but we can observe some of what Strauss aimed for in writing these scenes in such detail. Both men, as Strauss portrays them, are virgins at thirty-two years old.

Eng is the novel's narrator; he is literate, literary, always reading Shakespeare, and unhappier in their joined bodies than his much less discerning brother. Chang may not be as sharp as Eng, but he is blessed, initially anyway, with romantic love. He fell in love with Adelaide and desired to marry her. Eng and Adelaide's sister were lured into the double marriage for practical rather than romantic reasons. In fact, Eng is in love with his brother's wife, and it is Eng's ongoing desire for her that gives the sex scenes some of their excruciating poignance.

After describing kissing his own wife good night as the two brothers and Adelaide adjourn to the special, extra-large bed, Eng reports on the early stages of the encounter in great detail, including Adelaide's comment: "I've often wondered what this moment would be like. . . . Maybe I'm wicked. . . ."

I closed my eyes—the method Chang and I had decided upon—to become "mindless" for the next hour. But with each bounce or jolt or kick of Adelaide's leg, my eyes opened instinctively, as if against my will. . . .

And then my brother and his wife began to have relations.

Chang stirred me yet again as he climbed on top of his wife and me. He was touching her breasts at the nipples as if he feared he'd never get the chance again. My arm was wrapped around my brother's shoulder, and to make this positioning possible, our band extended farther than it should go. The inopportune logistics meant I had no choice but to curl against Adelaide, to cover her body partially—at the curve of her hip—and to move along her leg as my brother rocked back and forth. Chang saw my eyes were opened; he turned away quickly, and I closed them. As tightly as I could.

After some rolling of the three of us, Adelaide's soft blond hair came tickling across my neck, simultaneously gift and ordeal. I strained to keep my eyes shut as knees, elbows, fingers poked or bounced off me. Our band ached. Though my eyes were closed, I knew she was still on top of my brother because her hair gladdened my neck once again. I let my stare glide over her coloring face, following the swerve of bone in her exquisite cheek. Another accident, her fingers ran involuntarily against my palms before she could withdraw her embarrassed hand. She was alarmed and self-conscious and nearly crying. I felt alone and exposed.

Meanwhile, Chang, eyes closed, perspired, bit his lip, and then began triumphantly to smile. I felt something, too, like a feather dragged lightly across the length of my body, chin to feet, and I shivered. I began gradually, instinctually, I hoped imperceptibly, to approach the cheeks of my brother's bride with my own lips opened in an O. I cut their journey short at the last moment. The wind made a shrill noise through the magnolias outside, and the mattress sounded its own creaky song.

The scene is beset with temptation, denial, and torturous double messages. To be in bed with a woman you are forbidden to touch; to pretend you are not touching her when you are; to pretend you are insensate when you could not possibly be; to pretend you are not aroused—it might be better to be alone, never to know physical intimacy than to be tormented in these ways.

If what happens on a honeymoon is a preview of what is to come, that is no less true in this delicately constructed, anguished encounter.

LAST WORDS ABOUT NEWLYWEDS

Whether your fictional newlyweds are from the old world or the new, their honeymoon sexual encounters can tell us a great deal about what is in store for them, or, if they are looking backward, can dramatize what's been lost or gained. Either way, the weight of marriage gives these sexual encounters consequence. Even in our own time of sexual freedom, these can be important moments in fiction, with far-reaching repercussions.

7

LIFE SENTENCES: HUSBANDS AND WIVES

> Marriage is most often thought of as having little to do with eroticism.
>
> —GEORGES BATAILLE,
> *Eroticism: Death and Sensuality*

Sleeping with the same person every night for years means you have moved "out of the gutter of wild desire onto the smooth lawns of married love," as English novelist Fay Weldon said in her novel *The Loves and Lives of a She-Devil.* But take heart: *writing* about married sex can be every bit as thrilling as creating a torrid encounter between lovers who have yearned for each other across decades.

What could possibly generate so much excitement for a writer? The whole thicket of circumstances that in real life makes married sex predictable and familiar also gives you material from which to create conflict, expectations, disappointments, surprises—in other words, plenty of drama. If the couple has children, you have a built-in source of tension and intrigue. It can be almost as much fun as writing about committing adultery: *Do we have time before they wake up? Will they hear? Oh no, that's Susie at the foot of the bed.*

But with or without children, your married characters have a sexual routine. When you lead them into bed together, don't forget that as predictable as their moves might be to each other, they also have secrets, fantasies, desires, fears, and other distractions that they keep to themselves—and that *you* are in a unique position to let us in on. In real life, a lover's distraction can be a hindrance to intimacy, but in fiction, distractions can lead to conflict, misunderstandings, unrealistic expectations, and large and small disappointments. These are gems to be mined and polished.

And because married people share so much of life beyond sex, the rest of life can easily creep into their thoughts and deeds while making love, so that a sex scene can become a snapshot—more like a Polaroid—of a couple's life together.

This is certainly the case in a scene, too long to be included here, from the first chapter of John Updike's *Rabbit Is Rich*. After twenty years of marriage, Toyota dealer Harry Angstrom is more interested in reading *Consumer Reports* than in his drunk wife's advances. Once Harry relents and tosses aside the magazine, Janice tries to arouse him, but what gets him going are memories of a girl from ninth grade and a lover for whom he briefly left Janice many years before. Their few lines of dialogue are sadly revealing of the distance between them. Before their lovemaking goes too far, Janice passes out, though Harry is now aroused. He rearranges her body and decides to enter her from behind, so that "his prick is stiff as stone inside a sleeping woman. . . . Love has lulled her. Liquor has carried her off. Bless that dope. . . . He is stealthy so as not to wake her but single in his purpose, quick and pure." A sex scene between Harry and Janice Angstrom is a mini-history of their unhappy marriage.

In *Presumed Innocent* Scott Turow's narrator Rusty Sabitch spells out the limitations and burdens of married sex—the weight of history, all those quotidian distractions—by way of explaining his attraction to Carolyn Polhemus, whose murder he is charged with committing: "After almost twenty years of sleeping with Barbara, I no longer went to bed with only her. I lay down with five thousand other fucks; with the recollection of younger bodies; with the worries for the million things that supported and surrounded our life."

In these days of boundless sexual openness, an author's reticence can be more revealing than it was when *everyone* had to keep quiet about sex. In *Light Years*, a luminous novel about the slow disintegration of what seems like an ideal marriage, James Salter makes a sly, inaudible comment about the state of Viri and Nedra's sex life. In separate highly erotic scenes, we see both husband and wife make love with their respective lovers, but when they get into bed with each other, it is only to go to sleep.

Other fictional married couples, like many real ones, go to great lengths to keep their passions aflame, but none, I think, does it more ambitiously than the couple in Peruvian writer Mario Vargas Llosa's novel *In Praise of the Step-Mother*. Husband and wife are nightly aroused by telling their own erotic versions of classic myths based on well-known paintings. A glossy print of each painting is included in the novel, a sly gesture by the author: not only does he want us to see what inspires his characters, but he's inviting us to invent our own erotic tales.

GIVEN CIRCUMSTANCES

1. The characters have a complex shared history.
2. There is no drama inherent in married sex. People are usually not worried about being caught or leaving evidence, about who might have seen them enter the building and how much time they have left. In theory anyway, married sex is always available.

3. Couples may have a sexual routine, or go through cycles of passion, tenderness, distraction, or alienation. In any case, they are not likely to surprise each other with revelations about their sexuality or circumstances.
4. Nevertheless, they may have secrets, fantasies, and desires they keep to themselves.
5. Because they share so much of life beyond sex, the rest of life can easily creep into their thoughts *and* deeds while making love (as when Harry Angstrom can't stop reading *Consumer Reports* in *Rabbit Is Rich*).
6. Characters very likely feel comfortable and un-self-conscious with each other.
7. Characters with children may worry about waking them, or being disturbed or inhibited by them.

In a scene from Toni Morrison's *The Bluest Eye*, Pauline tells the erotic history of her marriage in a stream-of-consciousness style that seems closer to jazz or abstract painting than chronological narrative. She recalls, almost relives, the powerful but bittersweet sex she and husband Cholly had in the days before his chronic drunkenness. Now that she has two children and understands Cholly cannot support them, she has become a serious churchgoer and breadwinner, "an ideal servant," in the words of her rich, white employers whose house—unlike her own—is a source of pride to her. Occasionally she allows herself the pleasure of remembering those nights with Cholly:

> He used to come easing into bed sometimes, not too drunk. I make out like I'm asleep, 'cause it's late, and he taken three dollars out of my pocketbook that morning or something. . . . I think about the thick, knotty hair on his chest, and the two big swells his breast muscles make. . . . I pretend to wake up, and turn to him, but not opening my legs. I want him to open them for me. He does, and I be soft and wet where his fingers

are strong and hard. I be softer than I ever been before. All my strength is in his hand. My brain curls up like wilted leaves. . . . I stretch my legs open, and he is on top of me. Too heavy to hold, and too light not to. He puts his thing in me. In me. In me. I wrap my feet around his back so he can't get away. His face is next to mine. The bedsprings sounds like them crickets used to back home. He puts his fingers in mine, and we stretches our arms outwise like Jesus on the cross. I hold on tight. My fingers and my feet hold on tight, because everything else is going, going. I know he wants me to come first. But I can't. Not until he does. Not until I feel him loving me. Just me. Sinking into me. Not until I know that my flesh is all that be on his mind. That he couldn't stop if he had to. That he would die rather than take his thing out of me. Of me. Not until he has let go of all he has, and give it to me. To me. To me. When he does, I feel a power. I be strong, I be pretty, I be young. And then I wait. He shivers and tosses his head. Now I be strong enough, pretty enough, and young enough to let him make me come. I take my fingers out of his and put my hands on his behind. My legs drop back onto the bed. I don't make no noise, because the chil'ren might hear. I begin to feel those little bits of color floating up into me—deep in me. That streak of green from the june-bug light, the purple from the berries trickling along my thighs, Mama's lemonade yellow runs sweet in me. Then I feel like I'm laughing between my legs, and the laughing gets all mixed up with the colors, and I'm afraid I'll come, and afraid I won't. But I know I will. And I do. And it be rainbow all inside. And it lasts and lasts and lasts. I want to thank him, but don't know how, so I pat him like you do a baby. He asks me if I'm all right. I say yes. He gets off me and lies down to sleep. I want to say something, but I don't. I don't want to take my mind offen the rainbow.

As in Molly Bloom's stream-of-consciousness soliloquy in James Joyce's *Ulysses*, Morrison's presentation of Pauline's memories mimics her mental process, so we experience her thoughts and feelings with a startling immediacy. The intensity of Pauline and Cholly's sexual connection almost makes up for all they can't say to each other in words. But it is Pauline's awareness of the distance between them—at first, when she's pretending to be asleep and afterward, when she doesn't want to speak—that helps give this scene its melancholy edge. Even Pauline's fondest memories of making love with Cholly are tinged with disappointment.

One of the great pleasures of this passage for me is its varieties of language. Morrison mixes sexual bluntness and no-nonsense detail—*I be soft and wet; he puts his thing in me; he wants me to come first*—with lyrical metaphors, figures of speech, invented words, and religious references that transport us beyond the realm of purely physical sensation:

My brain curls up like wilted leaves.

The bedsprings sounds like them crickets used to back home.

we stretches our arms outwise like Jesus on the cross.

those little bits of color floating up into me—deep in me.

Then I feel like I'm laughing between my legs, and the laughing gets all mixed up with the colors.

And it be rainbow all inside.

Read the passage again and then refer back to the list of given circumstances. How many of the general truths about married sex has Morrison incorporated into this scene? How has she made them specific to Pauline and Cholly's lives?

In Stephen McCauley's fourth novel, *True Enough*, married sex is a source of conflict and comedy. Many years into her second marriage, Jane is dismayed and distracted by her young son's imperfections, her stalled career, and her growing boredom with her husband, Thomas, who is gentle and overly attentive, in contrast to her first husband, Dale, a slick, self-involved philanderer.

When Thomas embraces Jane in their kitchen on a hot summer night after their son has gone to bed, she thinks: "Oh please, don't get libidinous, not now, not tonight, not in this heat. . . . She immediately started to long for a small, harmless explosion somewhere in the house, a pipe bursting perhaps, something that would take hours to fix."

She has no such luck and a short time later they are in their air-conditioned bedroom, where Thomas prefers to keep the lights off, where "she could feel his fat, bloated penis bumping her, clumsily. It made her think of a Newfoundland puppy, a creature whose gawky, immature, undisciplined behavior was completely inappropriate to its size."

Nothing about this encounter is pleasing to her, and this is the source of the dramatic tension that propels the scene. She remembers her first husband's bold sexuality, their playful, open sex life, in sharp contrast to Thomas's "limited repertoire of moves," which "he always ran through in the same order, like a folk singer who plays the same songs in the same sequence."

McCauley dramatizes the distance between them by introducing some simple but meaningful dialogue:

"Is this all right?" he asked, more considerate and gentle than her gynecologist.

She managed a smile and nodded. "Mmmmm," she said. "Yes, it's fine."

A moment later, he asks the same question. Her answer, identical except in tone, leads to her long, revealing internal monologue that is a witty history of women's sexual mores:

"It's fine," she said, a little more sharply this time.

How had she come to this, a woman of her generation, brought up on the slogans of erotic liberation and revolutionary politics? She'd gone to nude beaches, smoked pot, used a vibrator, watched a pornographic video, and once, on a business trip, when she was much younger, had spent an afternoon in a Seattle hotel room with a total stranger. How had she ended up in an expansive burnt umber air-conditioned bedroom on a wide double-thick mattress, her hands limp on her husband's back, desperately waiting for his assault to be over, as if she were an icy Victorian hysteric? At least those miserable creatures didn't have to pretend to be enjoying it, didn't have to go through the humiliation of clenching and sighing and performing a grand finale as if she were a soprano bringing a big hammy bel canto aria to a predictably shrill close.

This sex scene serves three important functions in the novel: it dramatizes the dynamic of Jane and Thomas's marriage; it reveals the depths of Jane's unhappiness; and it prepares the reader for Jane's upcoming infidelity—with her ex-husband.

The scene, entirely from Jane's point of view, is an example of how bad sex can create a good sex scene. It also demonstrates that "bad sex" can be entirely in the mind and body of one individual. If this scene were from Thomas's point of view, it would likely be tender, romantic, and full of love that Thomas might not realize is not entirely reciprocated.

The secrets of husbands and wives are a common theme in scenes of married sex. This is the case with Dick and May Pierce in John Casey's *Spartina*, which won the National Book Award in 1989. Dick and May are not afflicted with an excess of desire for each other. Their long marriage is strained and beset with money problems. In this scene, Dick, a Rhode Island fisherman, has news he does not tell May about the fishing boat he is building. In the chapter immediately after this, Dick will take a lover, Elsie, who will help get him money to build the boat. His keeping a business secret from May foreshadows the more threatening secret he is soon to have.

Early one morning Dick comes home from a several-days-long fishing trip. May greets him, offers him breakfast, and, when he declines, makes a sexual proposition so noncommittal and dreary we might mistake it for small talk: "Well," she says, "why don't you go ahead and take your shower. The boys are out for the morning. I was going to clean some, but I can get to it later."

> He showered, came out in his towel, and took ahold of May's long waist. On the bed he slid her hairpins out the way she liked, even slower than usual, so it got to her more than usual, but all the while he couldn't get his mind off how he couldn't tell her what was going on on account of how right she'd been about Parker. He rubbed her slip on her skin the way she liked, feeling indecently competent as she breathed harder and got pink and hypnotized.
>
> Later on she said that she'd forgotten how much she used to miss him when he'd been going out regular on a boat. It was a nice thing to say, but it didn't reach him. He looked up at a thin spattering of rain across the windowpane, the tired southwester dragging on.

Most of the given circumstances of married sex apply here, all of them filtered through the lens of Dick and May's routine coupling. Their sexual pattern is down pat; seduction has been reduced to "I was going to clean some, but I can do it later." Once they begin, Dick uses several familiar gestures to arouse her. Rather than being carried away, all he feels is "indecently competent." Even the gloomy weather he notices out the window afterward reinforces the emotional staleness between them. And, of course, he's distracted by the secret he is keeping from her about the boat. Casey makes this sexual encounter with May important to the novel because it reveals to us the uninspired state of their intimacy, so that we are not surprised when Dick is susceptible to Elsie's entreaties in the next chapter.

This scene is a reminder to connect sex scenes to the total package of your characters' needs and wants and to the larger story, so that scenes do not feel "dropped in" and gratuitous. Because Dick's infatuation with Elsie is so central to *Spartina*, it is important we see the limitations of his sex life with his wife.

For couples with small children, married sex is often the sex that almost was—The Sex That Got Away. So it is for Lewis and Katie in Ron Carlson's short story "Plan B for the Middle Class." Married for fourteen years, they haven't had much sex since their sons were born three years ago. At last, they're leaving the kids with grandparents for a few days and heading for Hawaii: "I am one revolution of the earth away from the most astonishing sex carnival ever staged by two married people," narrator Lewis tells us. The only trouble is he has just been fired from his lucrative job writing a syndicated column on animal life (fundamentalist hate mail against evolution did him in), he hasn't told his wife yet, and he's got a nasty case of jock itch.

The night before they leave for Hawaii, they attempt a dress rehearsal for the carnival:

> The length of her body is the simple answer to what I am missing. It's an odd sensation to have something in your arms and to still be yearning for it and you lie there and feel the yearning subside slowly as the actual woman rises along your neck, chest, legs. We are drifting against each other now. Sex is the raft, but sleep is the ocean and the waves are coming up. . . . I run my hands along her bare back and down across her ribs and feel the two dimples in her hip, and my only thought is the

same thought I've had a thousand times: I don't remember this—I don't remember this at all. Katie sits up and places her warm legs on each side of me, her breasts falling forward in the motion, and as she lifts herself ever so slightly in a way that is the exact synonym for losing my breath, we see something.

There is a faint movement in our room, and Katie ducks back to my chest.

Their little boy is at the door, a reminder that there can be plenty of drama—great expectations dashed by the patter of little feet—in a sex scene between husbands and wives.

Once Katie and Lewis get to Hawaii, there are no children underfoot, but Carlson sets up enough obstacles, conflicts, and surprises—everything from a giant panda to a pair of young widows—to keep them from even being in the same room together for another twenty-three pages. Close to midnight, the carnival finally gets going:

> Now this next part, the bodies roll, their design made manifest, and there is achieved a radical connection. I'm not talking about souls. Who can tell about this stuff? Not me. You're there, you are both in something, something carnal and vaporish at once. Your mouths cock half a turn and you sense the total lock. You're transferring brains here; your spine glows. You go to heaven and right through, there's no stopping. What do you call it? Fucking? Not quite right here, this original touch, the firmament. My credo: you enter and she takes you in. This is personal. This is cooperation. Who can live to tell about it? You cooperate until you're married cell to cell, until all words flash away in the dark.

Lewis had promised us, and himself, an X-rated love fest, but what we get here instead is an astonishing piece of writing on the impossibility of describing sex and on its peculiar, total, and elemental power. If surprises are essential to a good sex scene, one of

Carlson's surprises here is how much the passage is about *ideas of sex.* His goal here isn't to put us inside his character's skin but to put us inside his head as he grapples with the conundrum of sex, with what sex is and isn't and what it should be called. Afterward his wife is sated and falls asleep immediately, but Lewis is up for hours more, wandering the hotel and the beach, remembering his high school graduation and the girl he was supposed to lose his virginity with that night. His Hawaiian sex carnival has become a history lesson in his own evolution, tying it to the human history of evolution, and those fundamentalists who try to deny it, and who cost him his job as a columnist.

Because married sex partners are so familiar to each other, because they are not making fresh physical discoveries the way new lovers are, a sex scene can have a more ruminative quality. While making love, a character has the luxury to wonder about the meanings and mysteries of the sexual connection.

Carol Shield's *The Stone Diaries,* which won the Pulitzer Prize for Fiction in 1995, is the inventive, collage-like diary of Daisy Stone Flett, an orphan whose life spans the twentieth century. Made up of eighty years of diary entries in the first and third persons, letters, photographs, and short-story-like narratives, Mrs. Flett reveals the sad truth about her sex life with her husband in a chapter called "Motherhood, 1947," under a heading she calls "Mrs. Flett's Intimate Relations with Her Husband." Because she "deeply, fervently, sincerely" wants to be a good wife and mother, she reads every issue of *McCall's* and *Good Housekeeping,* which even in 1947 are crammed with advice and letters from readers on sex. One reader asks if her husband's desire for sex every night is normal, leading Daisy to think:

> "[E]very night" would be a lot to put up with. Nevertheless she always prepares herself, just in case—her diaphragm in position, though she is repelled by its . . . yellow look of decay

and the cold, slick-smelling jelly she smears around its edges. It's a bother, and nine times out of ten it isn't needed, but it seems this is something that has to be put up with.

Mrs. Flett expects to perform her marital duties on nights before her husband leaves on business trips—"as a sort of vaccination, she sometimes thinks"—and when he returns. Here she imagines what might take place upon his imminent return after he has removed his trousers and tie:

> Then, unaware of her tears wetting the blanket binding and the depth of her loneliness this September night, he will lie down on top of her, being careful not to put too much weight on her frame. ("A gentleman always supports himself on his elbow.") His eyes will be shut, and his warm penis will be produced and directed inside her, and then there will be a few minutes of rhythmic rocking.
>
> On and on it will go while Mrs. Flett tries as through a helix of mixed print and distraction, to remember exactly what was advised in the latest issue of *McCall's,* something about a wife's responsibility for demonstrating a rise in ardor.

These passages are great fun to read, full of period piece detail, lovely juxtapositions, and unexpected sadness. They are excellent examples of how a sex scene, or an imagined scene, can reveal a great deal about character (Mrs. *and* Mr. Flett) and the sexual attitudes of the period. They reveal all this in a lively, original voice (Mrs. Flett's, being self-mocking), using details that locate us in the historical period and in the emotional desert Mrs. Flett wants to escape—but certainly won't, given the powers lined up against her (her husband and *Good Housekeeping* both). The passages and the period bring to mind Carolyn See's right-between-the-eyes line in her novel *Golden Days:* "I am speaking to you of the days when men did push-ups on your body and called that sex."

. . .

There are many events and circumstances that alter a married couple's sexual routine—altering the given circumstances as well—but none is more profound than the death or disappearance of a child, who exists, after all, because of this intimacy. A child missing, dead, or in serious trouble falls at the far end of a spectrum of child-related disturbances that can have powerful effects on a couple's sex life: everything from an infant's first fever to a teenager's first date.

Let's look at what happens in two recent novels in which parents have absent children too much on their minds.

In British writer Ian McEwan's *The Child in Time,* the loving marriage of Stephen and Julie Lewis shatters soon after their three-year-old daughter is stolen from a London supermarket during a few seconds when her father turned away from her. The child is never found; the parents separate. Stephen turns to drink and Julie to mysticism. She moves to the country and, two years later, while he is visiting her after a long absence, they end up in the bed that had been a wedding gift:

> The homely and erotic patterns of marriage are not easily discarded. They knelt face to face in the center of the bed undressing each other slowly.
>
> "You're so thin," said Julie. "You're going to waste away." She ran her hands along the pole of his collarbone, down the bars of his rib cage, and then, gratified by his excitement, held him tight in both hands and bent down to reclaim him with a long kiss.
>
> He too felt proprietorial tenderness once she was naked. He registered the changes, the slight thickening at the waist, the large breasts a little smaller. From living alone, he thought, as he closed his mouth around the nipple of one and pressed the other against his cheek. The novelty of seeing and feeling a familiar naked body was such that for some minutes they could do little more than hold each other at arm's length and say, "Well . . ."

and "Here we are again . . ." A wild jokiness hung in the air, a suppressed hilarity that threatened to obliterate desire. . . .

He wondered, as he had many times before, how anything so good and simple could be permitted, how they were allowed to get away with it, how the world could have taken this experience into account for so long and still be the way it was. Not governments or publicity firms or research departments, but biology, existence, matter itself had dreamed this up for its own pleasure and perpetuity, and this was exactly what you were meant to do, it wanted you to like it.

When their seventeen-year-old son Jacob is accused of murdering his girlfriend, Carolyn and Ben Reiser's world is permanently altered in Rosellen Brown's novel *Before and After*, a dramatic exploration of a parent's duty to shield a child from the consequences of his crime. The boy flees their small New England town and is apprehended months later in Cambridge, Massachusetts. After a chilling family reunion at the jail, during which Jacob does not say a word, Carolyn and Ben spend the night with friends in Cambridge—a successful couple with young children, a beautiful house, and a maid who cooks exotic meals. Since the police first came looking for their son, Carolyn and Ben have not made love. Late that night in the guest bedroom:

His hands were everywhere on her, every part of him awake and anxious. He didn't say a word.

She didn't resist. Confused, not sure whether this was a violation or his reading of a need of hers more secret than even she could acknowledge, she let him chafe her skin pink under his rough carpenter's hands and lay her back across the edge of the bed, where he pinned her desperately to the pink-and-green garlands on the sheets. He took no time with her, so that he had to rip his way in, and he howled when he came. He sounded like a man felled from behind by surprise.

She imagines the child in the next room hearing the howl and fearing that "someone—someone else" was being murdered. She moves away from her husband, glares at him, and says, "What a performance." She then accuses him of making so much noise as a way to assert himself, because over dinner the man of the house had been knowing and certain as to how they should handle their legal problems. Ben answers:

"You think that, hunh?" He closed his eyes and swayed a little like a man at prayer. "Won't anything ever be the same again? Carolyn? This will sound sentimental, I know, but—we're here in this—this normal house. I see these two people who can get into bed together at the end of the day like ordinary people and enjoy each other, make love like—friends, whatever you want to call it—and then turn over and go to sleep and not have dreams with battered heads in them and see the straps of electric chairs. . . . So I looked at the two of them, those two fucking lucky people, and I thought, That's what they're going to do when they go to bed tonight, they're going to think about us, poor schmucks who are in such trouble, and they're going to reach out for each other and celebrate their good luck. So I reached for you. So. I'm sorry."

When writing about a couple in these circumstances, keep in mind that the loss of a child is so powerful and consuming, you may not even have to mention it directly to make the reader experience the characters' anguish.

What separates a sex scene between characters with these burdens from other married characters?

• The couple's ordinary sexual routine has been so profoundly disturbed that when they do make love, it's a kind of "first time" for them. They are full of insights about the nature of sex (as in *The Child in Time*) or disturbing observations about their longtime partner (*Before and After*).

- They are in a heightened state of awareness, which is atypical of married sex.
- Sex now includes an element of drama—the missing child, the child in trouble—also atypical of married sex.
- The sex scene may also include feelings of guilt, ordinarily not associated with married sex: guilt at the pleasure they feel while their child may be in danger, guilt that they have not managed to protect the child. Pleasure becomes a kind of betrayal of loyalty to the child.

Then there are the innocent pleasures of prospective parenthood. This passage from John Cheever's classic first novel, *The Wapshot Chronicle*, published in 1957—a little too early for explicit sex between married characters—includes a delightful *reference* to married sex in the context of the romantic, affectionate evening on which Coverly Wapshot learns his wife, Betsey, is pregnant. After dinner she wants to go shopping for a chair in which to nurse their child. The passage conveys a degree of enthusiasm for sex atypical of the fiction of the period and leaves us with a strong sense of the tenor of the sex and the cozy state of intimacy between husband and wife:

After supper they took their walk. A fresh wind was blowing out of the north—straight from St. Botolphs—and it made Betsey feel vigorous and gay. She took Coverly's arm and at the corner, under the fluorescent streetlamp, he bent down and gave her a French kiss. Once they got to the shopping center Betsey wasn't able to concentrate on her chair. Every suit, dress, fur coat and piece of furniture in the store windows had to be judged, its price and way of life guessed at and some judgment passed as to whether or not it should enter Betsey's vision of happiness. Yes, she said to a plant stand, yes, yes to a grand piano, no to a breakfront, yes to a dining room table and six chairs, as thoughtfully as Saint Peter sifting out the hearts of men. At ten o'clock they walked home. Coverly undressed her tenderly and they took a bath together and went to bed for she was his potchke, his fleutchke, his notchke, his motchke, his everything that the speech of St. Botolphs left unexpressed. She was his little, little squirrel.

SOME FINAL WORDS ABOUT MARRIED SEX

The sex lives of married characters were strictly off-limits in fiction until the 1960s. Even D. H. Lawrence, who wrote explicitly about adultery in *Lady Chatterley's Lover* and sex between men and women who were not married in *Women in Love*, didn't reveal a thing about what went on between husbands and wives. The nineteenth-century European novels that shook with adulterous tremors—*Madame Bovary, Anna Karenina, The Red and the Black*—were silent about what went on in the marriage bed. Did authors keep mum because sex between their married but unfaithful characters was nonexistent, because it was uneventful compared to the extracurricular stuff, or because of a delicacy that honored the sacredness of marriage even as spouses violated their vows? We will never know, of course, but now that we have carte blanche to open the bedroom door on our married characters, we need more than ever to make it worth a reader's while. We know, after all, what goes on in there. It is the one place where sexual intimacy is officially sanctioned, where sex is *supposed* to happen. So the fact that it does is not particularly noteworthy, unless the author makes it so by creating a scene that tells us something essential about the nature of a couple's intimacy and what it has to do with the rest of the story.

8

THREE CHEERS FOR
ADULTERY

Adultery, Emma was discovering, could be as banal as
marriage.

—GUSTAVE FLAUBERT,
Madame Bovary

If adultery did not exist, writers would have had to invent it. It
offers a delightful spread of possibilities for conflict, high emotion, high humor, reversals of fortune, acts of moral turpitude,
and sex that's too hot to handle. Adultery provides its own plot
and narrative. The fictional lovers must maneuver and manipulate
to make their rendezvous happen; and later on they must often
clean up the wreckage from them. Just as important, from the
point of view of a writer who wants sparks to fly between more
than two characters, a single act of infidelity can involve an epic
and explosive cast: the two lovers, their betrayed spouses, friends
and colleagues privy to the deception, and unwitting, miscella-
neous witnesses.

When writing about married sex, as we saw in chapter 7, we often need to *create* tension and drama by plumbing the depths of our characters' psyches. But when the subject is infidelity, the drama is built into the encounter. Sometimes your best move can be to steer a hard course away from the predictable high emotion of it by creating characters who are blasé or unrepentant, as Tomas is about his chronic infidelities in Milan Kundera's *The Unbearable Lightness of Being*. Another very male, very British approach is explored in *Betrayal*, a play by Harold Pinter later made into wonderful movie with Ben Kingsley and Jeremy Irons. The men are good friends and colleagues and one is having an affair of long standing with the other's wife. The men go through elaborate motions of friendship over many years by completely ignoring the dangerous current that surges between them. Talk about tension, talk about subtext!

What else can a writer do with all the potential melodrama of adultery? Comedy. Once again, from my interview with Edmund White:

> Henri Bergson defined humor as that thing that happens when the material world resists the spiritual world. In other words, two lovers want to leave for their honeymoon, and they go out the revolving door and the door sticks. That's like the beginning of every *I Love Lucy* episode. In the same way, I think sex is a classic site for that kind of humor, because people have all kinds of extremely erotic ideas or romantic or passionate ideas about what they're going to accomplish in bed, and oftentimes it's a fizzle.

Leaven your adulterous scenes with humor, irreverence, and irony, as Joseph Heller does in *Something Happened*, in the excerpt on pages 140–41. Or give in to the drama of it and take us for a roller-coaster ride, as Scott Turow does in *Presumed Innocent*, in which the wife of a cheating husband kills his girlfriend and manages to frame her husband for the murder.

In our divorce-prone society, Alexandra Marshall's 1997 novel, *Something Borrowed,* offers a wry new twist to adultery: the illicit lovers are former husband and wife, who fall into bed together during the wedding weekend of one of their children. Each has married again; when they find themselves in a hotel room together, the woman notices herself in a mirror and thinks: "This wasn't adultery, though. This was a family reunion."

In real life we often hope our two-timing spouses will renounce their lovers and take the high road to domestic harmony, but in fiction, where conflict is critical, it's far more compelling when they don't. There would have been no stories to tell had Flaubert's Emma Bovary made do with dreary Charles and Tolstoy's Anna Karenina settled for a pallid marriage. Two of my favorite adulterers in recent fiction are husbands who can't give up the habit. Milan Kundera's Tomas is "genuinely incapable of abandoning his erotic friendships" and goes home to his wife's bed every night with his hair reeking of sex. In Fay Weldon's dark, funny fairy tale, *The Life and Loves of a She-Devil,* Ruth's accountant husband, Bobbo, takes up with his client Mary Fisher. Bobbo not only refuses to give Mary up, but insists on regaling Amazon-size Ruth with professions of love for petite Mary. His refusal to renounce Mary sets in motion Ruth's own wildly elaborate plan for revenge. Three cheers for adultery—when it leads characters and authors to these heights of invention!

GIVEN CIRCUMSTANCES

1. The sex is preheated—charged by its very nature—because the lovers meet in secret; there's typically an element of danger in being seen together and a time limit on the meeting. Urgency and deception can fuel eros.
2. Adulterers live at least three lives: the public, the married, the illicit.

3. Adulterous sex is compartmentalized.
4. Adulterers often compare the lover to the spouse. Lovers may solicit comparisons.
5. Adulterers try to conceal evidence—lipstick, body odor, restaurant receipts, or subtle changes in behavior and attitudes.
6. Emotions run the gamut from exhilaration and liberation to shame and remorse.
7. The romantic triangle has an inherent source of tension. If both adulterous lovers have spouses, possibilities for conflict, communication, and deception increase.
8. Desire for a person you can't have and don't know very well can take a long time to dissipate.
9. There's often an imbalance of power between adulterous lovers, with men usually in the lead. Society's double standards often judge cheating wives more harshly than cheating husbands. And with more married men than married women having affairs, men have more choices for partners than women do, again tipping the power in their favor.
10. Adultery is unpredictable, potentially explosive, and can lead easily to pain and dislocation for many—lovers, spouses, and children.

And yet, and yet . . . for the writer, as well as for lovers new to the beat, adultery is as seductive and sometimes as hard to kick as nicotine. Here's how English sociologist Annette Lawson describes its power in a 1989 study called *Adultery*:

Adultery, because it is secret, permits people endless variation. In adultery, each partner can make the lover represent anyone or anything—mother, father, sibling, superordinates or subordinates, angel or devil—with very little risk because, unlike marriage, adultery does not, at the outset, include permanence. Truth need never be revealed; the inadequacies of the reality of the self need never be demonstrated to the other. So long as the adultery is brief, the fantasy can endure. In this sense, adultery is far from dangerous; it is safe.

A character's attitude toward adultery, often a shadow image of society's view, can set the tone for an entire novel. When Anna Karenina and Vronsky finally become lovers, they are so riven by guilt and shame that he compares what they have done to committing murder.

These days, the power of shame to proscribe behavior isn't what it used to be. Mirroring society's attitudes, adulterous lovers who find their way to literature have little truck with the concept of remorse. For Bob Slocum, the amusingly tormented narrator of Joseph Heller's *Something Happened*, adultery is a fringe benefit of marriage. He even recommends it for his wife.

Though this monologue does not describe a sexual encounter, it illustrates how much mileage you can get out of giving your unfaithful characters well-defined attitudes toward adultery. In this case, Slocum's attitude is raunchy and irreverent, in keeping with Heller's tone throughout the novel.

My wife is at that stage now where she probably *should* commit adultery—and would, if she had more character. It might do her much good. I remember the first time I committed adultery. (It wasn't much good.)

"Now I'm committing adultery," I thought.

It was not much different from the first time I laid my wife after we were married.

"Now I am laying my wife," I thought.

It would mean much more to her (I think), for I went into my marriage knowing I would commit adultery the earliest chance I had (it was a goal; committing adultery, in fact, was one of the reasons *for* getting married), while she did not (and probably has not really thought of it yet. It may be that I do all of the thinking about it for her). I did not even give up banging the other girl I'd been sleeping with fairly regularly until some months afterward. I got four or five other girls up at least once those first two years also just to see for myself that I really could.

I think I might really feel like killing my wife, though, if she did it with someone I know in the company. My wife has red lines around her waist and chest when she takes her clothes off and baggy pouches around the sides and bottom of her behind, and I would not want anyone I deal with in the company to find that out. (I would want them to see her only at her best. Without those red marks.)

The juiciest surprise of this passage—following a trail of bread-crumb-size surprises about his sexual past—is Slocum's reason for not wanting his wife to sleep with any of his colleagues. Heller sets up the surprise by having Slocum tell us first that he would feel like "killing her" if she slept with a colleague. We expect him to elaborate with something like, "I couldn't bear to share my wife with the vice president of marketing." But instead of garden variety jealousy, he surprises us with what he feels are the humiliating imperfections of her flesh. Even in his fantasy of her unfaithfulness, he wants to look good with the guys at work.

There is also some ambiguity in Slocum's remarks. Because this statement occurs late in the novel, we know by now to take his most intimate feelings with a grain of salt, to look for the ways in which he is not being entirely candid with us or himself. It suits his tough-guy image to assert that the only reason he doesn't want his wife to sleep with someone in the company is because it might make him look bad. It's safer for him to joke about her body than to admit it would hurt his feelings for her to sleep with someone else.

• Whether you convey it directly or by suggestion, give us a sense of how your adulterous characters feel about the trust they are betraying. Are they guilt-ridden, blasé, sarcastic, and defensive, or—the untroubled few—blessedly content?

. . .

An upper-middle-class cheating husband who muses on the possibility of his wife having a fling has a quaint ring to it—like a Model A or a manual typewriter—in the cutthroat world of academic political correctness that Francine Prose skewers so wickedly in *Blue Angel.* The disastrous fallout from the single unconsummated act of adultery that married creative writing professor Ted Swenson—an ambivalent, first-time adulterer—commits with his best writing student, Angela Argo, is meant to suggest the ballad of Bill and Monica. Angela, too, wears thong underpants; Angela, like Linda Tripp, wires herself to collect evidence. The novel is a blistering indictment of feminism gone awry, of the balkanized world of gender and ethnic studies programs, and of puritanical sex-harassment mores.

The brief sex scene in Angela's dorm room is smartly written, politically correct (Angela is comfortably sexually aggressive and produces a condom from her night table), and it exemplifies the comic principle that bad sex can make a very good sex scene. A paragraph into things, "there's an explosion inside his head. A crack, a crunch, and then a grinding, like stone turning to powder." Angela heard it, too. Swenson's tooth has broken.

> This is dreadful! Unfair! At the moment he's been longing for and denying he wanted, when at last he gets what he hasn't dared to dream, he cracks a tooth. How middle-aged, how pathetic to be unmasked as a geriatric case with emergency dental problems! Still connected to Angela, Swenson moves his tongue to the back of his mouth and probes the jagged ruin.
> "I lost a filling," he says.
> "That's not all you lost," says Angela. . . . "Bummer," she says. "Does it hurt?"

It is quite a bummer for Swenson, especially a few weeks later, when Angela files a sex-harassment complaint against him, setting in motion the complications that it takes the rest of the novel to resolve. The incredible guilt he feels toward his wife, whom he's been faithful to for their long marriage, becomes a distant luxury once he's put on leave from his job and spends his time drinking and reading "the great classics of adultery, or, depending on one's personal interpretation, the great classics of inappropriate, tragic, ennobling, life-changing love. . . . Passion and its punishments: poison, prison, a train. Not much slack for sinners."

Blue Angel is a novel of ideas, and the sex scene is interesting for its breezy smartness and humor, and for all it sets in motion. This is a world in which sex matters intensely, matters, that is, to the lockstep ideologues in power who think that it should be uniformly regulated, regardless of circumstances—regardless of the complex truths about human desire.

The adultery in Erica Jong's classic novel of women's liberation, *Fear of Flying*, explores the politics of sex and sexuality before the new Puritanism took hold. Jong's Rabelaisian heroine, Isadora Wing, has just come to "that inevitable year when fucking [your husband] turned as bland as Velveeta cheese." Rather than leave the marriage, she searches for an uncomplicated, anonymous fling, what she calls "the Zipless Fuck." Enter Adrian Goodlove, a British psychoanalyst Isadora meets while attending a convention of analysts in Vienna with her analyst husband, Bennett.

Those who go to the trouble—and take the risk—of committing adultery understandably have high hopes for their illicit assignations. The higher their hopes, the further they have to fall when plans go awry. To the cheating lovers, mechanical failures or logistical impediments can be devastating, but to a writer interested in crafting a compelling sex scene, there's nothing like a lost car key or a little impotence to subvert the predictable. Isadora may not be having a good time in this scene, but her creator certainly is.

After necking with Adrian Goodlove in a parking lot, Isadora is convinced he is a prime candidate—her first live wire—for a zipless dalliance. A day later, she's in his hotel room:

> In his room, I stripped naked in one minute flat and lay on the bed.
> "Pretty desperate, aren't you?" he asked.
> "Yes."
> "For God's sake, why? We have plenty of time."
> "How long?"
> "As long as you want it," he said, ambiguously. If he left me, in short, it would be my fault. Psychoanalysts are like that. Never fuck a psychoanalyst is my advice to all you young things out there.
> Anyway, it was no good. Or not much. He was only at half-mast and he thrashed around wildly inside me hoping I wouldn't notice. I wound up with a tiny ripple of an orgasm and a very sore cunt. But somehow I was pleased. I'll be able to get free of him now, I thought; he isn't a good lay. I'll be able to forget him.
> "What are you thinking?" he asked.
> "That I've been well and truly fucked." I remembered having used the same phrase with Bennett once, when it was much more true.
> "You're a liar and a hypocrite. What do you want to lie for? I know I haven't fucked you properly. I can do much better than that."
> I was caught up short by his candor. "OK," I confessed glumly, "you haven't fucked me properly. I admit it."

When she admits she had been afraid to be honest with him, he surprises her by saying that his ego isn't as fragile as she had imagined. When she says she has never met anyone like him, his answer is far from perfunctory: "No, you haven't, ducks, and I daresay you never will again. I told you I'm an antihero. I'm not here to rescue you—and carry you away on a white horse." Is he being profound or just defensive because he couldn't perform? Whatever his motivation, his retort about not rescuing her on a white horse is germane to the rest of the novel and to her internal struggles: how Isadora can make peace with her desires for sex, love, fame, creative fulfillment, security, and independence. Adrian's offhand remarks throw the central issues of the novel back into her court in ways she could not have anticipated.

Like all true heroines, Isadora has decided what she wants, gone after it, been thwarted—and keeps on plugging. Her setback is only temporary. Even after this encounter with Adrian, she still wants to find bliss and transcendence with him; she won't quit for another two hundred pages.

After the brief paragraph that summarizes their disappointing sex—so unsatisfying that Jong just touches on the low points, rather than re-creating each stroke—she skillfully keeps the scene going by making Adrian the dominant character, the character who does not accept Isadora's statements at face value and challenges every one of them, creating conflict and causing her to face up to her own dishonesty and her own illusions.

The scene turns on two surprises:

1. A surprise of action: the zipless fuck can't get it up.
2. A surprise of character: though Adrian has failed her test for potency, he has passed "a character test" she had not even meant to administer. Unlike Isadora, he is willing to talk honestly, take responsibility for his actions (and failures to act), and to confront her with insights she would rather avoid.

Some of the tension and energy in this scene come from the fact that Isadora and Adrian go to bed together with vastly different expectations. She is embarked on a major marital/psychic experiment; he is just looking for a good time. When the machinery doesn't work, he can say to himself, and to her, "Better luck next time." But for Isadora, the mechanical glitch shatters a fantasy she has counted on to rescue her from the doldrums of her marriage. It makes great sense that Adrian can bring insight and observation to the encounter that Isadora cannot: he sees it for what it is—a romp with a near stranger—not a magic potion for a woman in the midst of a crisis.

- Adultery is a high-stakes gamble in which both partners are not often satisfied equally because expectations and disappointments tend to run to extremes. Make sure at least one of your characters wants something very specific from the exchange, make sure we know by the end of the scene whether he or she has gotten it—and also what it might have cost him or her, in pride, self-esteem, or sexual identity.

The mood is mournful and elegiac in this scene from Russell Banks's novel *The Sweet Hereafter.* Narrator Billy Ansel, a young widower, is recalling everything that led up to the school bus accident in which his twins and twelve other local children were killed. His former lover, Risa, and her husband, Wendell, own a motel; their child was one of those killed. Before the accident, he and Risa met regularly in Room 11 of her motel while a baby-sitter took care of his twins. The accident brought an end to the affair, but while it was going on he would sit in the dark motel room waiting for her:

It sounds sordid, I know, but it didn't feel cheap or low. It was too often too lonely, too solitary, for that. Many nights Risa could not get away to Room 11, and I sat there by myself in the wicker chair beside the bed for an hour or so, smoking cigarettes and thinking and remembering my life before Lydia died, until finally, when it was clear that Risa could not get away from Wendell, I would leave the room and walk across the road to the lot next to the Rendez-Vous where I had parked my truck and drive home.

On those nights when Risa did arrive, we spent our time together entirely in darkness, for we couldn't turn on the room light, and we barely saw each other, except for what we could make out in the dim light from the motel sign outside falling through the blinds: rose-colored profiles, the curve of a thigh or shoulder, a breast, a knee. It was melancholy and sweet and reflective, and of course, very sexual, straightforwardly sexual, for both of us.

Our meetings were respites from our real and very troubled lives, and we knew that. Whenever I saw Risa in daylight, in public, it was as if she were a wholly different person, her sister, maybe, or a cousin, who only resembled in vague ways the woman I was having an affair with.

The loveliest and most instructive surprises of this scene are Banks's use of the motel and of the darkness, separate elements that he fuses together to great effect. Having Billy Ansel's married lover own a motel gives Banks the opportunity for the two to betray her husband on his own property, an extra-dangerous and extra-treacherous gesture.

The fact that Risa shows up sometimes and not others—and that Billy waits in the dark for her—adds to the precariousness of the relationship, and the sadness. Looking back at the relationship through the prism of the accident and the children's deaths magnifies the sadness of the affair a thousandfold.

But what looms largest and most hauntingly in this scene is the darkness in which they make love, and the glancing slivers of light that illuminate disparate body parts. The darkness is a necessary part of their camouflage, but Banks uses it as almost another character in the scene—the character who gives them permission to have their straightforward sex with no emotional attachments or complications; they can't even read each other's faces. Their sex has the single-mindedness, and limitations, of masturbation; it doesn't pretend to be about anything other than feeling good.

Though Banks gives us no explicit details, the combination of the darkness, the rose-colored outside light tinting the flesh, and two people hungry for each other without restraint, apology, or pretense adds up to a surprisingly erotic scene. The reader knows enough about the setting and the mood so that when Billy tells us their sex was "very sexual, straightforwardly sexual," we are almost challenged to fill in our own private details, making the scene as erotic as our imagination allows it to be.

The setting of an adulterous sex scene—everything from the lighting to the landscape—can be a powerful element in heightening the level of illicitness and intrigue. Because the lovers are not supposed to be where they are, the setting itself is forbidden, an accomplice in the rendezvous. It can give you almost as much energy and information to work with as another character.

SOME LAST WORDS ON ADULTERY

Adultery can be a source of high drama and upheaval, farcical comedy, or of quiet, anguished intrigue. For a writer, a sexual triangle founded on deception is blessed with its own high-stakes narrative: Will the lovers' secret life be revealed? Will the marriage or the love affair win out? Will the betrayed spouse find out and forgive? Will the jilted mistress retreat with dignity or boil up her lover's child's pet rabbit for dinner, as Glenn Close's character does in *Fatal Attraction*?

Whether your cheating-hearted characters get caught in flagrante or nearly implode in their efforts not to, be sure that the action of your story is driven as much by who your characters are and what they want as by the inherent drama of adultery.

9

YOUR PLACE OR MINE: RECREATIONAL SEX

He was not exactly as handsome as he had been the night before—no man ever is—but he was still pretty superb, and he was ready.

—CHRISTOPHER COE,
Such Times

We had been lovers only because we had attached no importance to love; but we felt the most sincere friendship for each other.

—GIACOMO CASANOVA,
The History of My Life

In other chapters of this book we've looked at sexual encounters through the prism of the relationships of the people who have them: virgins; spouses; adulterers. The beneficiaries of "recreational sex" are—pick your terminology—dating, sleeping around, getting acquainted, falling in love, hooking up, picking up, or engaging in what Milan Kundera calls "erotic friendships." They are not betraying a spouse, a cause, or an internal or external set of moral strictures with their passion. They are looking for intimacy, closeness, love, and a good time, which may last five minutes or long enough to bring the new person home for Christmas. This is sex without history, without guilt, and, to shifting degrees, without commitment. Before the sexual revolution this species of pleasure was available only to men, artists, bohemians, and Europeans. Today, we are all eligible, even though AIDS has brought an end to the bravado of the 1960s and 1970s.

What does all this (mostly) unencumbered frolicking mean for fiction writers?

Writing about recreational sex is kind of like having it: the sex is the main event, and though it lacks the inherent drama of the illicit, it offers other possibilities for excitement and connection. Unlike married sex, it has no history and no certain future; it can lead anywhere or nowhere. The stakes are not inherently high, at least at the beginning, though they may become so faster than anyone intended. In his first novel, *An American Romance,* John Casey captures the paradoxical nature of casual sex, to some extent of all sexual encounters—that people can be physical intimates but emotional strangers—when his main characters, Anya and Mac, two graduate students at the University of Chicago, make love for the first time and drift off to sleep with Mac thinking: "He wished he knew her well enough to speak."

Without furtiveness, history, or a future to focus on, the writer must use the encounter to some or all of these ends: to give us information about the characters; to give us a status report on the relationship, on the role and meaning of sex in it; and, through the dialogue, voice, interior monologue, and details, to offer other insights into characters or into the narrator, as James Salter does with his voyeuristic narrator in *A Sport and a Pastime.*

The transformation from casual sex to deepening intimacy is articulated movingly in this passage from Joseph Olshan's *Night-swimmer,* set in gay New York in the 1990s:

The first feast of another man's body is both joyful and confusing. I want to fill myself with everything, every nipple and biceps and every inch of cock, but I want to savor it and that demands more than one occasion. When I know a man for a while, when the parts of his body become familiar to me, as his own scent that I carry on my clothes, on my forearms, when he ceases to become just a name and becomes a familiar man, that's when the real sex begins. By then he's told me private things, and I know something of his story; and when I reach over to touch him in a bed that we've both slept in night after night, nothing casual, no matter how galvanic, can rival the power of that touch. For that touch is now encoded with the knowledge that I could lose everything, and movement by movement, as I make love, I'm more completely aware of what I stand to lose.

One of the most talked about examples of sexually explicit writing from the last few decades is Harold Brodkey's short story "Innocence," first published in 1973 (a good year for recreational sex). The story of two seniors at Harvard, the narrator, Wiley, falls in love with a beautiful woman, Orra ("to see her in sunlight was to see Marxism die"), who, though she has had lovers for six years, has never had an orgasm. If casual sex often leaves writers with a lack of conflict for their characters to act out, "Innocence" is shot through with dramatic tension: almost every time they make love, Wiley is determined to make her come and she is determined to resist. For twenty densely written pages, they battle it out between the sheets (he wins, of course). Brodkey captures for us every physical and psychic flutter that passes between them (just as he instructed Edmund White to do when he wrote his own sex scenes). It's too long and too tightly written to be excerpted here. It appears in his collection *Stories in an Almost Classical Mode*.

GIVEN CIRCUMSTANCES

1. Unless the characters are friends who fall into bed together, the characters probably don't know each other well.
2. They have few if any commitments to each other or to anyone else.
3. They have individual sexual histories but not a common one.
4. They may have other sex partners currently in circulation.
5. They may be sexually uninhibited but emotionally guarded.
6. They may have vastly different expectations of the encounter.

An awareness of divergent expectations plagues the plucky narrator of Pam Houston's story "How to Talk to a Hunter," in which a single woman is drawn again and again to a man who is trouble and who ropes her in with sex and a rugged exoticism. Written in the second person, she is full of self-mockery and self-effacement over this Great Western outdoorsman who, on their first night at his place, asks if she wants to sleep under "skins or blankets." She tells us: "You will spend every night in this man's bed without asking yourself why he listens to top-forty country. Why he donated money to the Republican Party. Why he won't play back his messages while you are in the room. . . ." Why can't she give him up? "The sun on the windows will lure you out of bed, but he'll pull you back under. The next two hours he'll express what will seem to you like the most eternal of loves. . . . Even in bed; especially in bed, you and he cannot speak the same language."

Her best friends tell her the hunter is bad news; he has other girlfriends; he's evasive; when she tells him she loves him, he answers, "I feel exactly the same way." But she cannot resist:

Play Willie Nelson's "Pretty Paper." He'll ask you to dance, and before you can answer he'll be spinning you around your wood stove, he'll be humming in your ear. Before the song ends he'll be taking off your clothes, setting you lightly under the [Christmas] tree, hovering above you with tinsel in his hair. Through the spread of the branches the all-white lights you insisted on will shudder and blur, outlining the ornaments he brought: a pheasant, a snow goose, a deer.

These teasing but virtually chaste sexual encounters fit perfectly with the narrator's guardedness, the hurt she is trying to rewrite in the face of the hunter's continuing rejection. She feels vulnerable, afraid of expressing her feelings because she knows they will not be returned, and so is doing what she can to control the situation: keeping up a snappy patter, constructing a polished surface to hide the emotional turmoil underneath, letting us know she knows she is being mistreated—and that she has what it takes to handle it with panache. It would have been out of character for her to reveal too much more of herself in a graphic sex scene, given how much she has already exposed of her unreciprocated and ill-advised longings.

- Recreational sex often begins with both partners feeling carefree and uncommitted, which is not a good omen for creating dramatic conflict. Conflict develops when one character's feelings move at a different pace, and in a different direction, from the other's, as happens quickly in this story.
- You can keep conflict going, as Pam Houston does here, by involving characters outside the relationship, as when the woman consults her friends for advice.
- There is nothing more important in revealing who characters are than specific details in dialogue and description.

The narrator of Jane DeLynn's very smart and sassy novel *Don Juan in the Village* is always on the prowl, looking for love, sex, and adventure in places where "women like me"—lesbians—are welcome: Key West, Ibiza, Italy, L.A., bars in downtown New York. The variety of sexual episodes is vast, and the narrator is self-effacing, ironic, and wonderfully observant. She enjoys her escapades as much for the cheap thrills and outside possibility they may lead to love as for the stories they will give her to tell years later. In our interview DeLynn observed that what is erotic is "obviously in the realm of the mind." The workings of her narrator's mind play a keen role in her sex scenes.

On a trip to Italy in the early 1970s, where the narrator has gone to recuperate from a deep depression set off by her apartment burning down, she encounters a wealthy, older Italian man with a "young and beautiful" girlfriend "who did not confine her sexual interests exclusively to persons of one gender." Their three-way rendezvous takes place in the woman's apartment, where Carlo and Francesca proceed to undress the narrator and turn her slowly around:

> I found this impersonal inspection of my body extremely arousing. The American women I had slept with were either lesbians who were still embarrassed by their attraction to women or feminists who pretended that the reason they slept with women was not sexual but ideological; this casual acceptance of the carnality of our transaction seemed to me the essence of European sophistication.

A few minutes later, Carlo and Francesca

> seemed fascinated by my great wetness. I explained to them I had had *una problema* and had been unable to make love for a long time and now that I could it was very exciting. The word *"problema"* seemed to upset Francesca and I tried to explain that the kind of problem I meant was of the head rather than the body, that my apartment had burned down and I had become sick—that is, tired—of the life. They looked at me uncomprehendingly. . . . I felt happier and more comfortable

than I had in ages—partially on account of the revival of my sexual desire, but even more, I think because of the exoticness of the situation. I imagined both the story I would tell my friends and the one I would write about this . . . [and] I liked not understanding what was being said.

After Carlo and Francesca have intercourse, she observes that Francesca was more excited by Carlo than by herself:

I realized, with the slight surprise that always accompanies such revelations, that there really were women who liked men better than women—better even than a woman as remarkable as myself. It occurred to me I might have been brought there less for Francesca's sake than for Carlo's.

These passages are wonderful examples of the two-things-happening-at-once principle: on the surface, they tell the story of a casual menage à trois between virtual strangers. Had DeLynn stuck to describing the three-way mechanics, the scene could have read like instructions for assembling a jungle gym. But the narrator's comments and observations fill out the encounter and add these elements:

• Conflicts between characters and between cultures.
• Revelations about the narrator's feelings and vulnerabilities that probably were not apparent to Carlo and Francesca.
• A historic dimension, which locates us at a time in history, the early 1970s, when the collision of the women's movement and the lesbian rights movement made sexual encounters between women politically loaded in the ways that DeLynn's narrator describes.

The sexual ambience in English writer Alan Hollinghurst's novel, *The Swimming-Pool Library* is intense, compulsive, not at all restrained, except in the writing, which provides a chilling counterpoint to the characters' sexual abandon. It tells of the sexual peregrinations of William Beckwith, a young, directionless, gay aristocrat during the summer of 1983, "the last summer of its kind there was ever to be" before AIDS made its mark on sex habits in England. Though the novel seems at first loosely plotted, driven almost entirely by the sexual urges of Beckwith and his far-ranging, biracial set (gay men from sixteen to eighty-three), a more complex architecture emerges, and the story extends its ambitions dramatically, putting each sexual encounter not only into the context of England's treatment of gay men throughout the twentieth century, but using the plight of gay men as a symbol of state-sponsored and condoned bigotry.

In my letter to Hollinghurst, I asked this question: "AIDS hovers over the narrative. Did its lurking presence make you feel any sense of defiance or abandon in writing the sex scenes?" Here is his answer:

> I planned the book in the earliest '80s, and even when I started writing it at the beginning of 1984, AIDS, though already a major thing in the U.S., had hardly begun to be comprehended in Britain. . . . Then, in November 1984, a close friend of mine in London died of it; and over the following months I had to make a decision as to whether or not to incorporate into the novel a recognition of this disease which was so grimly altering the very world that much of the book was about. In the end, as you know, I decided to set it firmly in the hot summer in 1983; but of course the book took on a newly historic character that I could not have foreseen when I first imagined it. And yes, the outburst of anti-gay hostility that followed the arrival of AIDS did make me all the keener to write about gay sex in an unapologetic way.

The Swimming-Pool Library is such a brilliantly integrated novel, I hesitate to pull out a scene or two for demonstration purposes.

Though each sex scene is superbly well written, the cumulative effect of them has even greater power. Beckwith shuttles between encounters with live-in or steady lovers and with strangers in movie theaters and clubs. According to an entry in his best friend's diary, Beckwith always picks men who are "vastly poor, & dimmer than himself—younger too. I don't think he's ever made it with anyone with a degree. It's always these raids on the inarticulate." One such raid is on Arthur Hope, an unschooled seventeen-year-old black man who, after a week of passion with Beckwith, is now hiding out in Beckwith's apartment after killing someone. Beckwith is torn between wanting to protect him, love him, and throw him out in order to reclaim his apartment and his privacy:

> We barely used language at all to communicate: he sulked and thought I was putting him down if I made complicated remarks, and sometimes I felt numb at the compromise and self-suppression I submitted to. . . . But then in sex he lost his awkwardness.

On another occasion not long after, Beckwith is again fed up with the burden of Arthur's presence and the disturbing power of his attraction to him:

> My whole wish was to throw things around, make a storm to dispel the stagnant heat, assert myself. Yet I found myself fastidiously tidying up, tight-lipped, not looking at him. He followed me helplessly around. . . . He was confused, wanted to be ready to do what I wanted, but found he could only annoy me further. Then I hurled the stack of newspapers I was collecting across the floor and went for him—pulled the trousers down over his narrow hips without undoing them, somehow tackled him onto the carpet, and after a few seconds' brutal fumbling fucked him cruelly. He let out little compacted shouts of pain, but I snarled at him to shut up and with fine submission he bit them back.

Afterwards I left him groaning on the floor and went into the bathroom. I remember looking at myself, pink, excited, horrified, in the mirror.

A few minutes later, Beckwith goes back to Arthur, cradles him, and tells him how much he loves him. He then tells us,

There were several occasions of this kind, when I was exposed by my own mindless randiness and sentimentality—our affair had started as a crazy fling with all the beauty for me of his youngness and blackness. . . . I saw him becoming more and more my slave and my toy, in a barely conscious abasement which excited me even as it pulled me down.

This scene is convincing and compelling for many reasons:

- The writing is vivid, precise, and full of unflinching, unflattering candor and insight about the narrator and Arthur, whose very lack of speech is a large part of his character, and one of his appeals to Beckwith.
- The sexual encounter—actually more of an attack—occurs in the context of the entire unequal relationship and mirrors it with an accuracy troubling to Beckwith. He has every social advantage over Arthur; sexual domination is the final hold he can have over him, and he exerts it. Sex for Beckwith is as much an assertion of power and class as it is of pleasure. The irony is that even Beckwith's pedigree as a member of the aristocracy does not protect him from the prejudice and violence he suffers elsewhere in the novel because he is gay.
- At the heart of this and other sex scenes in the novel is Hollinghurst's exploration of the complexities and contradictions in our urges for sex, intimacy, and autonomy.
- The direct, matter-of-fact language of the sexual encounter matches the nature of the sex as well as the narrator's blunt, almost confessional attitude toward his actions.

• In sex scenes involving characters whose connection is primarily sexual, who have no particular responsibilities to each other, and do not know each other well, a narrator or main character who keeps trying to understand his partner, or understand the nature of his attraction to his partner, as Hollinghurst does here, can add tension, complexity, and insight to a relatively hollow encounter.

The last gasps of the AIDS-free sexual revolution—from a different vantage point—were also an influence in my first novel, *Slow Dancing,* set around the election of Ronald Reagan in 1980. I conceived of the story as being about two sexually liberated thirty-year-old women, best friends, who wanted to abandon the emotionally empty, often furtive, casual sexual relationships they had craved during their twenties and trade them in for something more stable and less secretive. The novel came to be about the failure of sex to give my characters the emotional connections they slowly came to admit they wanted. I was also keen to explore the sleight-of-hand that is in the nature of lovemaking: the promise, often dashed, that the intimacy of the moment will last beyond the finish line.

The book opens with Lexi, a lawyer for the poor, on her way to dinner with a man who will become important to her. As she drives, she remembers her early days as a lawyer and lover to Stephen Shipler, an older, slick lawyer, a distant, icy man to whose chilly charms she was oddly susceptible. During the first sex Lexi has with him, she is completely focused on the mechanics. She is so out of touch with her emotions that it is not until the next morning when he leaves her that she allows herself to feel anything. Even then she is more comfortable sizing up Shipler to see what she can learn from him than admitting she might have feelings for him. The first night:

In his hotel room he used his hands to hold her head, moved it with deliberate but tempered force—far more than a suggestion—from a spot on his neck to his chest to himself. He kept his hands pressed firmly to her ears, then played with strands of her hair. He moved her head then away from himself so that he could feel her breasts there, between her breasts, and he pressed them close around it, which no one had ever. . . . It was weird having it pushed into her face, pushed against her, as casually as if it were a finger. He was so sure of himself. So cock-centered. The phrase had never occurred to her before that moment, when it was locked between her breasts.

When he was inside of her later, she felt the same taut, sure strength in his hips as they pressed into her, forcing her to press back. . . . With his hips he pulled her along to the edge of sensation and then let her pull back ever so gently, and back and forth and back and forth. She felt as if she were getting ready for a dive, jumping up and down on the end of the diving board to get a feel for the springs. Tighter than she had expected. Though she offered no resistance and came right before he did.

When they caught their breath and pulled the covers back up, Stephen kissed her on the cheek, a quick good-night kiss, and rolled over and slept by himself.

The next morning, she pretends to sleep while he packs; they say good-bye blandly and he departs:

Lexi turned over, drew the cover up around her and thought: How many women has he left like this in hotel rooms? A bit surprised by the cheap drama of the thought, and how it had come to her full-blown, like a jingle from a commercial or the refrain of a song, mass-produced and ready for consumption by the brokenhearted. She was a little brokenhearted, but she was also intrigued by the constellation of circumstances: his law-firm smooth, his odious charm, his cock. The wallflower gets laid by the captain of the football team and even though she knows it's not love—and it may not even be romance—it's its own sort of triumph. . . .

There were some things she wanted to learn from Stephen Shipler. One of them was . . . taking what you want when you want it, which seemed to be one of the things he did best.

In this scene, the casual sexual encounter is woven into the narrative so that it has an effect on the character. In this case, it causes Lexi to change her behavior (take up with Stephen for her own chilly reasons) and perceive herself differently (as someone who can choose lovers for their practical, not sentimental, value). The encounter provokes a multiplicity of reactions and leads ultimately to the tough-talking attitude that Lexi professes in the novel's opening line.

The only choice I regret, reading over the scene more than fifteen years after I wrote it, is the "himself" in the opening paragraph. I don't remember what inspired this lapse into coyness in my otherwise unabashed narrative. It doesn't work because "himself" is not what Lexi thinks while this is happening. "Himself," prudish and indirect as it is, would be a fine choice if it were the word the character used or thought when considering that part of the anatomy.

In her novel *Waiting to Exhale* Terry McMillan deals deftly with the "himself" issue—as well as contraceptives and AIDS protection—without naming names. In an early scene between Robin, one of the four girlfriends who narrate the novel, and her pudgy new suitor, Michael, McMillan captures the narrator's sassy blend of experience, curiosity, anticipated disappointment, and blustery longing while making the sexual stage directions an integral part of the narrative. Robin takes off her sweater and bra, Michael's eyes bulge with appreciation, and he slips under the covers with his boxer shorts still on

before I got a chance to see what he had to offer.
"I knew you were going to be beautiful all over," he said, after I got under the covers. "And you smell so good." He

put his little fat hand over one of my breasts and squeezed. My nipples immediately deflated.

"Do you have protection, or should I get it?" I asked.

"Right here," he said, pulling it from the side of the bed. He took his shorts off and threw them on the floor. Then he put his hands under the covers, and his shoulders started jerking, which meant he was having a rough time getting it on.

"Do you need some help?" I asked.

"No no no," he said. "There." He rolled over on top of me, and since I could no longer breathe, let alone move, I couldn't show him how to get me in the mood. He started that slurpy kissing again, and I felt something slide inside me. At first I thought it was his finger, but no, his hands were on the headboard. Then he sort of pushed, and I was waiting for him to push again, so he could get it all the way in, but when he started moving, that's when I realized it was. I was getting pissed off about now, but I tried to keep up with his little short movements, and just when I was getting used to his rhythm he started moving faster and faster and he squeezed me tight against his breasts and yelled, *"God this is good!"* and then all of his weight dropped on me. Was he for real? I just kind of lay there, thinking: Shit, I could've had a V-8.

This scene works in part because Robin comes to it with a specific ambition: she is interviewing this guy for the position of lifelong companion, after a long history of unsatisfying relationships. She comes to it with both an expectation *and* an attitude: sassy skepticism. The conflict and comedy arise from the clashing of her huge ambition for the occasion, her jaundiced attitude, and poor Michael's merely human fumblings.

Sex is Robin's way to judge the worth of the man and the future of the relationship, certain that if he cannot satisfy her sexually, she cannot count on him to satisfy her emotionally. She is prepared to call it quits and cut her losses, but moments later Michael surprises her by soliciting her feelings, asking what she wants from life, and expressing his fondness for her. When they make love again a short time later, she manages to forget that he's fat, short, and pale. Instead of accentuating the comedy of the encounter, she allows herself to tumble to the unexpected emotional warmth of it.

- When your characters come to sexual encounters with different expectations, these differences lead to friction, conflict, and, in some cases, comedy. All you need to know as you begin to write a sex scene is what *one* character's expectations are. Conflict sets in when the other character can't or won't give her what she wants.

Max and Nora, the lovers in Glenn Savan's novel *White Palace*, are an unlikely pair, well suited, it seems, only in the sack, where their differences set off enough sparks to send the Space Shuttle into orbit. He's a bookish, ambitious twenty-seven-year-old Jewish widower; she's a forty-one-year-old, tough-talking, hard-drinking, Reagan-loving White Palace waitress. Nora has kept any number of secrets from Max, the darkest about her son Charley, who, she told Max, died of leukemia. When Nora's sister Judy visits—the first time they have seen each other since Charley's funeral—Judy reveals the truth to Max, that he died at fourteen of a drug overdose, horribly neglected by both parents. Max does not mention this revelation to Nora. This scene takes place that night, with Max and Nora sleeping in the living room and the visitors in the bedroom. (We've learned before that Nora has gynecological problems and can no longer conceive.)

Nora entered the living room naked, a bad idea with guests in the house, and from the weave of her walk he could see how drunk she was. She got into bed beside him and turned unceremoniously upon her back. Max wasn't sure if this contained a sexual invitation or not. Such complex passivity on her part was unknown to him—except for those times when he started things rolling by applying his mouth to her. This he began to do, swiftly losing himself in the flowery complexities of her labia, until her thighs tightened in refusal and she sat up, taking his face between her hands. "Just fuck me," she said.

She lay back down and waited.

"Right now?"

"Yes."

She waited stoically, like a good Victorian wife. She felt abnormally tight as he entered her. And then there was a further surprise; she was silent. He thought this might be in deference to Bob and Judy down the hall, but that didn't explain what her eyes were doing open, or why the look in them was so liquid and beseeching.

"Max," she said, just as he was starting to come apart against his climax. "Max, I have to tell you . . ."

"What?" he managed to say.

"I just wish . . ."

"What?"

"I just wish we could have a baby."

For an irrational moment he wished it too. And then he spurted his useless seed.

The details of their sex life are well documented in the novel, so that when we come to this scene, several months into the stormy affair, we know how different it is from earlier encounters; Max takes note of all the differences and wonders what accounts for them, which creates a bit of dramatic tension. Though told from Max's point of view, by the end of the scene we can well imagine what has been going through Nora's head since her sister's arrival that she has not shared with Max: a replay of her son's death and the troubled life that led to it. The author uses the scene to reveal the ongoing anguish that Nora feels about her son but cannot express except when lovemaking lowers her defenses. The scene also shows us—and Max—that Nora feels much more than a sexual connection with him, while Max can only allow himself a momentary fantasy of that kind of commitment to her.

• You can make a sex scene a turning point in your story when your characters do or say something especially revealing while making love.

The highly erotic and finely chiseled sex scenes in James Salter's *A Sport and a Pastime* fall technically in the category of "recreational sex" but could as easily find a place under "voyeurism" and "fantasies." Doing triple duty in this way gives the scenes an emotional richness and an intense sexual charge that draw one back to the novel again and again.

Set in France in the early 1960s, it tells the story of a pair of young lovers, a twenty-four-year-old Yale graduate named Dean who takes up with a young French shop girl, Anne-Marie. Occasionally Dean reports on the affair to a male friend, another young American, our narrator, who is traveling through France, studying its history and architecture, and imagining and recreating for us the details of Dean and Anne-Marie's affair. Infrequently the narrator reminds us that this is *his* script, not the transcript of Dean and Anne-Marie: "I am not telling the truth about Dean, I am inventing him. I am creating him out of my own inadequacies, you must always remember that." But of course we often forget it, as the author means us to, because the love scenes are so staggeringly real, which keeps adding to our sense of the narrator's loneliness. He has nothing to do but wallow in fantasies of *someone else's* affair. These fantasies are *his*, projected onto Dean—the safest sort of fantasies to have.

For example, in the scene that occurs before the one quoted below, Dean has talked to Anne-Marie about all "the ways to love, the sweet variety." When she asks what they are, Dean cannot say, though eventually we, and Anne-Marie, are meant to understand that the one he is most curious about is anal sex. Toward the end of the scene below, the mention of lubricants—and "frightening" evidence—refers to this:

> She is in a good mood. She is very playful. As they enter her building she becomes the secretary. They are going to dictate some letters. Oh, yes? She lives alone, she admits, turning on the stairs. Is that so, the boss says. *Oui.* In the room they undress independently. . . .
> "Ah," she murmurs.
> "What?"
> "It's a big *machine à écrire.*"
> She is so wet by the time he has the pillows under her gleaming stomach that he goes right into her in one long, delicious move. They begin slowly. When he is close to coming he pulls his prick out and lets it cool. Then he starts again, guiding it with one hand, feeding it in like line. She begins to roll her hips, to cry out. It's like ministering to a lunatic. Finally he takes it out again. As he waits, tranquil, deliberate, his eye keeps falling on lubricants—her face cream, bottles in the *armoire.* They distract him. Their presence seems frightening, like evidence. They begin once more and this time do not stop until she cries out and he feels himself come in long, trembling runs, the head of his prick touching bone, it seems. They lie exhausted, side by side, as if just having beached a great boat.
> "It was the best ever," she says finally. "The best . . . We must type more letters."

Were this scene a faithful account of the goings on of Dean and Anne-Marie, it would be an impressive—and juicy—piece of writing. But it would lack the haunting, melancholy, self-punishing quality it has as the narrator's fantasy.

Reread the scene and take note of these elements:

• This is a fantasy within a fantasy; the narrator is imagining Dean and Anne-Marie acting out a fantasy (his fantasy).

• There are few adjectives or adverbs throughout.

• The scene is not dropped into the narrative but made to connect with what comes before, notably Dean's interest (read: the narrator's interest) in anal sex, which he wants but is ashamed to pursue.

• The writing, in part, has a pornographic intention and intensity: its primary purpose is to arouse the narrator. Its secondary purpose is to make us understand—indeed, *feel physically*—the intensity of his longing, loneliness, and shame.

It's easy to see that voyeurism and fantasy can be powerful elements in your characters' sexual encounters, but they are far more interesting if you can connect them to thematic and narrative issues in your work. In *A Sport and a Pastime*, a lonely narrator becomes a voyeur and fantasist, creating narratives so immediate that we forget he has invented them, just as the author of the book has invented *his* stories. Might we all be voyeurs?

LAST WORDS ABOUT RECREATIONAL SEX

There is nothing sweeter than the freedom to have sex without guilt or remorse, whether it is with your spouse of thirty years or a ragingly handsome new lover. As a fiction writer, that freedom means you will have to work awfully hard to create compelling sex scenes. Without internal or external dramas to stoke the engines that fuel essential conflicts, you have to know your characters thoroughly, create clear distinctions between them, and exploit those differences with all the creative tools in your arsenal: your imagination, sense of drama, ability to empathize with your characters—and your determination to rewrite until you get it right.

10

THE ILLICIT: SEX FORBIDDEN BY LAW, HISTORY, AND POLITICS

> The Lord God took the man and put him in the garden of
> Eden to till and keep it. And the Lord God commanded
> the man, "You may freely eat of every tree of the garden;
> but of the tree of the knowledge of good and evil you shall
> not eat, for in the day that you eat of it you shall die."
> —Genesis 2:15–17

Stepping out on a spouse isn't our only chance to sample the
fruits of forbidden sex. In fact, adultery is pretty tame next to the
sparks that can fly when characters violate laws and taboos
beyond their marriage vows. Love that takes hold and thrives in a
hostile environment is a rich, complex source of material for a
writer, full of built-in sexual tension and possibilities for political,
legal, and psychic repercussions. Forbidden sex can fuel a plot;
give your characters a secret life to lead; define the atmosphere of a
novel—of an entire historical period—and bring police, secret
and otherwise, into the boudoir, if only via tape recorder and
camera. Beyond the immediate advantages for the writer of work-

ing with characters who defy laws and conventions, on occasion a particularly hearty character becomes a symbol of resistance or liberation to readers who are similarly oppressed.

When England was a particularly hostile environment for homosexuality—Oscar Wilde was jailed for two years in 1897 for homosexual activity; working-class homosexuals were routinely hanged in the nineteenth century—all a fictional character had to do was spend the night with someone of the same sex to become a hero or role model to generations of gays and lesbians. In *The Well of Loneliness*, British author Radclyffe Hall's description of her heroine's first lesbian sexual encounter (on page 316 of 447 pages) is limited to these few prim words: "and that night they were not divided," but these were enough. Soon after publication in 1928, the novel was banned (until 1948). E. M. Forster, by then well known for *A Room with a View* and *Howards End*, published twenty years earlier, campaigned against the banning. His own fiction involving homosexual characters, including the novel *Maurice*, was not published until after his death in 1971 and was greeted even then by American writers and critics with condescension and homophobia.

Times change and so do hostile environments. Nathaniel Hawthorne's Hester Prynne would not have to wear her scarlet "A" today; copies of *Ulysses* are no longer seized by U.S. Customs agents; and British playwright Joe Orton's scandalously risqué dialogues of the mid-1960s are as inoffensive as La Rochefoucault's aphorisms if compared to the daily fare served up on afternoon TV. Apartheid is officially over and so is the Cold War, but for a writer with a nose for strange fruit, there are still stories to tell about sex that is forbidden by law, by convention, or by history.

GIVEN CIRCUMSTANCES

Many of the same given circumstances of adulterous sex (see chapter 8) apply here as well, minus, of course, the betrayed spouse and the web of complications accompanying that deception.

1. The sex is preheated, charged by its illicit nature.
2. Lovers typically meet in secret; there's danger in being seen together and often a time limit on the meeting.
3. Because of the danger, lovers are often in a heightened state of awareness.
4. Characters who indulge in forbidden sex have secret lives.
5. Like adulterers, the characters may try to conceal evidence of their liaisons, not from a spouse but from a parent, sibling, coworker, authority figure—anyone who might take offense at or action against their behavior.
6. Guilt may accompany feelings of exhilaration, liberation, rebelliousness, or, particularly in the case of gays and lesbians in a hostile environment, relief at no longer having to conceal their secret selves.
7. Context is everything. The writer must paint a vivid picture of the society or culture that forbids the sex to dramatize how much is at stake for the characters who violate its laws and conventions.
8. Sex scenes between illicit lovers often include references to the outside forces that would rather keep the lovers apart.

EXAMPLES

There's more relief than satisfying sex when two lonely gay men arrange to meet in a beachside changing shed in "Contact," a short story by Australian writer John Lonie. After communicating anonymously for several days via public toilet graffiti—"the tribal calling card"—the story's forty-year-old narrator slinks to the bushes with the young man whose handwriting was on the toilet stall wall. Both are vacationing in Australia with their respective families (parents, grown siblings), far from the comforts of gay-friendly cities. The narrator, who spends most of the holiday minding his young nieces and nephews—in a role he calls "the modern version of the family aunt"—pegs his cruel four-year-old nephew Hans a "poofter-basher [gay basher] in training." Out of loneliness, horniness, and feelings of separation from his "tribe" in the city, he takes a gamble on the anonymous invitation. But instead of the toilet stall veteran he expects, a nervous seventeen-year-old who looks even younger shows up, bringing an intense, bittersweet reminder of the culture's "poofter-bashing" laws and attitudes.

The story concludes with their meeting, which the narrator intends to flee once he sees how young the young man is:

I am about to say you're too young for me and I'm too old for you when I feel him trembling under my touch and he puts his hand up to my hand and presses it against his cheek. My heart melts. He's scared, so scared he's shaking, and I realize that it is he who's taken the huge risk, not me. I fold him in to me and hold him and he hangs on tightly, so tightly.

His erection hasn't gone away and then he shudders and grabs me hard as I feel him come against my thigh. I hold him tight and press my face to his, stroking the back of his neck and head. Then I feel dampness on my cheek and he's crying softly. It's okay, I say quietly, hoping he feels safe with me, cry all you want. And he does.

For ages, we stand here, him hanging on tight. I can hear his heart beat and the sound of the blood coursing through his veins, this stranger. I should be looking after him, not that little thug Hans or any of my nieces and nephews. They've got their parents. This one, he's my tribe, that's for sure. Who looks after him? Who looks after any of us at that time?

. . . I tell him how brave he is, taking such a chance. So are you, he says, we're illegal up here, you know. Not "it's" illegal but "we're" illegal. He is so lonely, so very lonely, you can taste the need on his skin.

Multiply him by thousands and what other way is there than the change rooms or a public toilet whose doors become a *samizdat?* And when as strangers we collide in that fleeting moment, the immensity of feeling between us creates such a closeness that we go on searching for it, desperate just once more to taste the sweetness it brings. It surely is the kindness of strangers.

This narrator follows his urge for an anonymous fling and ends up with far more than he bargained for—ends up, in the way of all good fiction, being surprised by the distance between what he wants and what he gets. The desire for anonymous sex is selfish and simple, but the pursuit of it—even a pursuit as single-minded as this one—forces unpredictable elements into the mix: the needs and frailties of other human beings. Had the narrator gotten exactly what he set out for, a beachside bacchanal, there would have been no surprise, for him *or* for us. And not much of a story to tell.

In a scene about illicit sex, as in this one, one or both characters may feel more fear than sexual excitement—fear of admitting what they are doing, fear that they will be caught, exposed, and punished. As you reread this scene, pinpoint places where one character expresses fear and the other acknowledges it. The author goes on to use that emotion to propel the scene forward and convey the legal and political climate that *causes* the fear.

- The more fearful character is comforted by the narrator, whose own apprehensions have been overshadowed by the boy's.
- The narrator acquires a soothing strength in relation to the boy, instead of feeling, as he did at first, like a sexual predator.
- The boy's fear leads the narrator to reflect on his place in his family and culture and to realize where he must direct his allegiance.
- The last paragraph moves from the personal to the political with the narrator's comparison of the writings on toilet doors to *samizdat,* highlighting the risk men are taking as well as the noble cause of free expression they assert in these messages.

. . .

Older men and teenage girls, or even younger—Vladimir Nabokov did not invent the appetite, only gave us the name Lolita for the syndrome. In the two movies that have been made from the novel, the actresses have been shapely teenagers, but in the book, Lolita is a prepubescent twelve-year-old, weighing seventy-eight pounds. Humbert's obsession is with a scrawny child. Nabokov's obsession is with language, not sex. In fact, Humbert would just as soon skip the details of their coupling. In 1955, when the novel came out, after years of being turned down by publishers, the subject matter was so shocking that scenes of explicit sex would have prevented its publication altogether.

Readers were as shocked by Humbert's unabashed hunger for the twelve-year-old daughter of his rooming-house landlady, later his wife, as they were by Lolita's casual complicity in these crimes against her. The density and rhythms of Nabokov's prose are those of a man panting, a man, as Humbert describes himself while sitting with Lolita, "in a state of excitement bordering on insanity." The prose rocks with suppressed desire; with desire that can't be suppressed; with whimsical, witty, cutting plays on words. But as for the physical details of their copious couplings, Humbert always prefers the clever suggestion to the excessively explicit— and well he should; he is recounting these events from his jail cell. Why draw more attention to the nature of his crimes than he has already been forced to acknowledge? His grandiloquent account of his first time with Lolita:

> Frigid gentlewomen of the jury! I had thought that months, perhaps years, would elapse before I dared reveal myself to [Lolita]; but by six she was wide awake, and by six fifteen we were technically lovers. I am going to tell you something very strange; it was she who seduced me. . . .
>
> I shall not bore my learned readers with a detailed account of Lolita's presumption. Suffice to say that not a trace of modesty

did I perceive in this beautiful hardly formed young girl whom modern co-education, juvenile mores, the campfire racket and so forth had utterly and hopelessly depraved. She saw the stark act merely as part of a youngster's furtive world, unknown to adults. What adults did for purposes of procreation was no business of hers. My life was handled by little Lo in an energetic, matter-of-fact manner as if it were an insensate gadget unconnected with me. . . . But really these are irrelevant matters; I am not concerned with so-called "sex" at all. Anybody can imagine those elements of animality. A greater endeavor lures me on: to fix once and for all the perilous magic of nymphets.

The Cold War made sleeping with the enemy something of an occupational hazard for generations of Western diplomats and military men stationed in Communist countries. Once the Wall came down, it wasn't only the authors of Cold War thrillers who had to find new enemies for their heroes to slay; sex across international borders lost some of its dangerous edge.

In the days when it was still razor sharp, the male lead in my novel *Safe Conduct* (1993), diplomat Eli "Mac" MacKenzie, got involved with a young Russian woman, Lida, while working in the U.S. consulate on assignment to Leningrad in 1974. Though married at the time, he and his wife, who remained in the United States, had an open marriage in which they even told each other about their love lives. Once he returned to the States, Mac and Lida were both punished by their governments for the affair and forced to stop communicating. Seventeen years later, after the Berlin Wall came down, Lida, now living in the West, calls Mac and they arrange to meet. The catch is that Mac is now married to a new wife, Kate Lurie, who knows the story of Mac and Lida; she accompanies him to the reunion; and, as narrator of the novel, she remembers and reimagines the story Mac told her years before, at a time when Lida's reappearance in his life was as remote as the collapse of the Soviet empire.

Using Kate to narrate these events gives the story and the sex scenes a multiplicity of dimensions. The sex scenes can be about far more than what goes on or went on between the lovers.

Here's part of Kate's re-creation of Mac and Lida's first night together in bed in his Leningrad apartment. (Earlier Mac told Lida that his apartment is bugged; Lida told him that "the Komitet" is Soviet slang for the KGB.)

> "And your wife—are you sure she'll be happy you're in bed with me?"
>
> "Lida, I don't want you to think that this might turn into something else, I—"
>
> "Come on, I'm kidding. Don't be so serious all the time."
>
> "But I am serious." He did not mean to sound stern. He ran his hand down the length of her voluptuous torso. "Serious about this."
>
> "You are, aren't you." It was not a question. She stretched her back against the bed. "Very serious."
>
> "And this."
>
> She nodded, made a faint sound that came from the back of her throat. Her back arced, her legs fell open. When he looked up at her face, eyes shut, cheek hard against the pillow, he noticed a small scar. For a few seconds it distracted him. Then her hips began to rock, and he was surprised to hear her speak. "Let's give them something to remember."
>
> "Who?"
>
> "The Komitet. And everyone else who's listening."

Later in the novel, while at Mac's apartment, Lida calls a friend from high school who works for the KGB, just to be sure she can get in touch with him, in case she needs protection: she is taking a risk sleeping with a U.S. diplomat, who is automatically considered a spy by the KGB. After the phone call she asks Mac what she should do if the KGB contacts her and asks about her relationship with him. "'You can tell them anything I've told you,'" he answers. They are about to leave for a bar; she is going to borrow a shirt of his. Again, this is Mac's point of view as reported and re-created by his new wife, Kate:

The rules here are meant only to keep you off balance, keep you guessing about where the real danger lies. It's everywhere, isn't it? That's what they want you to think. Maybe it's true. But whoever is listening on the headphones, labeling and cataloging the reels of tape—this is the only conclusion they will be able to reach: Lida and Mac are practically starved. She turns to ask about the shirt she will borrow and it is no more than the startling aquamarine of her eyes that draws him across the room. She undoes his pants with one hand and the buttons of her blouse with the other. What thrills him more than any specific sensation is the blunt fact of her desire. She wants this as much as he does. . . . She kneels and rubs her nipples against his knees, her tongue to the crease of his scrotum. He will tell [his wife] her name, that he met her in a restaurant, that her father is in the military, but how can he possibly tell her that beneath the eyes of the secret police, a love affair with every single sigh on tape—How can he tell his wife that in this country of vast, unspeakable sorrows, where the newsreels of his childhood, the Siege in the dead of winter, play around the clock, he is happier than he has been in years?

Though neither scene is especially graphic, both depict oral sex: cunnilingus, in the first example, fellatio, in the second. In both, the moments of sexual contact are compressed and much less direct than either any slang or any more clinical description I could have used. Instead, in both cases, I have made the reader work a bit to figure out whose body parts are where. Also, instead of focusing on the progress of the sexual activity, I focus on the characters' awareness of being watched by the KGB. I allow the characters to be turned on by this, but I also mean for the reader to remember, with a bit of a jolt, that it is Kate narrating and inventing the scenes. The reader might conclude (as I meant her to) that Kate feels both threatened and aroused by her own inventions; and that she has taken the place of the KGB in her paranoia and voyeurism.

• When writing about sex in a police state or under surveillance, the presence of other eyes and ears on the scene, and in the scene, can lead the characters toward fantasy and voyeurism in their sexual exchange.

In a situation where a government tries to use sex to blackmail its adversaries, you can get a lot of mileage out of weaving politics into sex scenes and sex into political scenes, as Julius Lester does deftly in his novel based loosely on the life of Dr. Martin Luther King Jr., *And All Our Wounds Forgiven* (1994). It's set in the present and told by four characters looking back on the turbulent 1960s, including the wife of slain civil rights leader John Calvin Marshall, his young blond mistress, Elizabeth, and Marshall himself, speaking to us (in lowercase letters) from the great beyond but wise to all that's happened in the years since his assassination.

The night after leading a major civil rights march in Washington, D.C., Marshall is summoned from the hotel room he's sharing with Elizabeth to the office of the FBI director, a dead ringer for J. Edgar Hoover. This political confrontation has a strong sexual component and is essential to our understanding of the times, of Marshall's character and commitment, and the context for his intense sexual connection with Elizabeth. The FBI director is the first to speak in Marshall's account of the event:

"i listened to that speech of yours yesterday and it made me sick. . . ."

he had a folder in front of him and shoved it across the desk at me.

"what do you think the american people would say if they saw some of those pictures? i've got tapes, too. i'll say this for you: you can make the bedsprings squeak."

i opened the folder to see a grainy photograph of a naked elizabeth astride the naked me. beneath it there were more: she with my penis in her mouth, me with my head between her legs, me atop her, me entering her anally.

there was such a welter of emotions: embarrassment, shock and anger and outrage that i had no privacy anymore. yet i was also fascinated. we all have photographs of ourselves at picnics, family reunions, weddings, graduations. but we never have the chance to see ourselves making love. part of me wanted elizabeth to see the photos and to reminisce with her about where we had been in this photo and where in that one.

behind the photos was a sheaf of papers, a log of the motels and hotels in which we had made love. i knew we made love a lot but seeing it documented that way, i couldn't help but be impressed.

The director then tells Marshall that unless he withdraws from political activism, he will send copies of these photographs to the press *and* to Marshall's wife. Marshall's answer: "do you need any help licking the stamps?"

This is a confrontation between good and evil, between a man of unlimited power and no scruples and an underdog with a just cause. The surprise here for Marshall is to find out that even while making love, he cannot escape his public self; that his enemies are prepared to use everything, including his sexual appetites, to extinguish his commitment to justice. The surprise for the reader in this scene is Marshall's unexpected delight in this package of explosive evidence meant to be used against him.

This is not, of course, a sex scene, but a scene in which we see a corrupt government trying to use sexual activity as a weapon of control.

• In writing about people under surveillance or people subject to black-mail, the blackmailers can become characters in your story, whether or not they actually meet the people they are attempting to control. But if they do, confrontations are a dramatic opportunity for victims to learn their private lives have been monitored and confront their opponents face-to-face.

Sex and politics need not be played for such high stakes to create disturbances in the field. In British writer Roger King's darkly erotic novel *Sea Level*, his characters' attitudes toward sex are essential to the story. It is narrated by a malcontented economist, Bill Bender, whose international consulting work takes him to troubled Third World countries where he is supposed to improve living conditions for the poor, but who is estranged from his wife, a sexually repressed, upper-class French woman, Mireille. When a colleague—a determined, straight-talking Chinese woman named Han—asks if she can accompany him on trips to the Third World, as a way to gain the necessary experience to get promoted from "statistical assistant" to "professional staff," he is ripe for the asking:

She was intelligent, knew the work, went straight to the point. Unlike genteel Mireille, she was most at ease naked, her knees fallen apart; she liked it in the light, in dangerous places. She had an energy, a hunger; we were formidable. My father, I felt sure, would sense the wantonness in her, the absence of niceness and be appalled. I liked that too, the break of it, the shedding of all that slavish fear, respect for betters, all that settling for half a loaf. She didn't ask me to be dutiful, didn't claim my obedience with hers; she only invited me to take her on. Or so it seemed to me.

I had said in my office that night [when she asks if she can accompany him on trips], playing to her script, "And what will you do for me?" She had played it mock Chinese, pulling her schoolgirl glasses down her nose with a calculated winsomeness: "Suk yor kok?" She had me then. I was lost then.

Bender's comparisons of his wife to Han are as much an attempt to understand the women as to understand his own attraction to them, his dual desires to play it safe and to court danger. With Han on a trip to Liberia, he goes along with her brazen exhibitionism.

I look, though Han does not, at the face of the old woman pressed against the window of our car. She is poor, one of the ones Han wished us to be among while we did this. The woman may be nearly blind, which could be why she's approached so close; I can't tell from the blankness of her eyes. Han is not looking at the woman but is twisted back to look at me. She wears only a blouse, which is undone. She's on my lap and I'm still high up inside her; her hand is still in place underneath herself. She ignores the old woman, a hand's length away, whose inexpressive eyes sweep back and forth over us. On our side of the glass the temperature is comfortable. On the old woman's side it is more than a hundred degrees. We are in Liberia. Han has twisted back to me, the little wry smile on her face, somehow pleased. I look from the old woman with her flaps of empty breasts pressed up against the door—surely the metal is burning her flesh—to Han's wry smile. Though I can't hear her, she has just said, "That was weird!" in a tone of deep gratification. I am definitely with Han.

Bender tells us later that he felt excitement as well as disgust, "either at the act or the fool she made of me." Such is the power of sex that it can drive us to commit acts that offend others, put us in danger, and mock and belittle our avowed ambitions, in this case, to help the poor of Liberia.

• In order to make a character's exhibitionism believable, as Han's is, the author must establish traits beforehand that suggest behavior so public might flow from the character. Because Bender acquiesces, we must, and do, know enough about him beforehand to find his actions credible, too.

The narrator of *The Final Opus of Leon Solomon* by Jerome Badanes is an Auschwitz survivor and a scholar of Jewish history who is about to commit suicide. In New York City in the 1980s, Leon Solomon is tormented by his past—his parents' early deaths, his sister's murder by the Nazis in the streets of Warsaw, his time in Auschwitz, his failed marriage—and certain of a bleak future after being caught stealing pages from Jewish documents in the Forty-second Street Library and selling them to the Harvard Judaica Society; he will be barred forever from libraries. He checks into a hotel of faded splendor and, on a stack of yellow legal pads, composes his final opus: the story of his life.

The Final Opus has surprised many readers in its sexually explicit scenes, almost all having to do with forbidden sex: the near-incest between Leon and his severely arthritic sister as they try to pass for Aryans in Nazi-occupied Warsaw; sex the Nazis force on young Solomon and a prostitute as they watch; and the torrid, three-night affair between Solomon and his neighbor in New York City, Kirstin Dietrich, the daughter of a Gestapo officer, around the time he was stealing from the library.

During their hiding in Warsaw, Solomon came close to making love to his sickly younger sister; he regrets now that he didn't. "That restraint of mine was a crime against my doomed sister. I consider that lack of defiance against the Nazis, and against God, too, if you will, my gravest sin." His other crime against her was that he did not poison her before the Nazis beat her to death and left her in a public square, "to instill terror in any Poles still harboring Jews." In the world that Hitler made—and that Badanes re-creates in his novel—certain acts of incest and murder are a kind of grace. His sister had been a promising concert pianist crippled as a young teenager by arthritis.

Every night after that I carefully soaped Malkele from her long graceful neck down to each and every toe. Though her limbs were atrophied and her spine bent slightly backwards, her small breasts remained girlish and as lovely as her face. Soaping Malkele, slowly, gently, quietly, became for us our kaddish for our obscured childhood and for our dead mother and father. This soaping was our only defense against the looming Nazi death machinery. During the day we longed for those few moments of slippery tenderness. My own muscles craved it as much as hers.

Yes, yes, we were, after a fashion, Malkele and I, lovers. But we obeyed the final taboo—we never, to be cold and German about it, fornicated. I washed her hair. She still cursed and threatened me. I soaped every inch of her body. I caressed her pointy nipples with the palm of my hand. I dried her and helped her into her nightgown. I carried her to her bed. I brushed her thick reddish black hair in the candle-lit bedroom. Once she whispered to me, "To what are Chopin's Preludes preludes?" and I kissed her. Sometimes after that, I lay with her. We kissed each other's lips and we embraced, but I never entered her. That restraint, which I adhered to religiously—Malkele, I am sure, would have welcomed me, though even she was never bold enough to ask . . .

If we should omit these most private details from the historical record, there is no way to appreciate fully the richness of

life for two young Jews, surviving temporarily, with false iden-
tifications as Pavel and Maria Witlin, on the Aryan side of
Nazi-occupied Warsaw.

For Solomon, the need to go into such explicit detail and
thereby create a "historical record" is both personal and professional. He is compelled to establish a record of his sister's life and
death in order to come to terms with his own guilt and, as a histo-
rian, in order to replenish the records and lives destroyed by the
Nazis and the Diaspora.

• In scenes of illicit sex, at least two things, if not more, must be happening at once: sex and politics, sex and history, sex and defiance.

The cost of sexual passion plays a prominent role in the abundant
fiction of Joyce Carol Oates. Nowhere is it more prominent or
more forbidden than in a novella set at the turn of the century in
upstate New York, *I Lock My Door Upon Myself* (1990). It is the
story of the forced marriage of an ethereal woman named Calla to
a brutal older man. As the result of violent, combative sex, she
bears three children and then manages to refuse her husband's
entreaties. In a turn of events that shocks her family, her community, and people for miles and generations, she falls in love with
Tyrell Thompson, a black man who comes to their house as a
water diviner, looking for hidden water deposits with a forked
twig. He is the first black she has ever seen and she identifies
immediately with the separateness his race imposes on him: *"Like
me they are outcasts in this country. No not like me: they are true
outcasts."* Her husband tries to kill her, the townsmen bind Tyrell's
legs and hurl him in a river (he survives: *"As if it was true, what
he'd always boasted—water was his friend and in his power"*). She
becomes pregnant with his child and finally abandons her family.
Tyrell asks her to row downstream with him in an old boat he

has found "on a day when anyone might see them who chose to see, setting their course deliberately for the falls at Tintern that had not the power—so he boasted, or gave the air of boasting—to withstand Tyrell Thompson's God-given mastery over water."

When they make love moments after he asks her to do this, they are rougher than usual. Calla is startled by the lack of ceremony and afterward she

> lay dazed, tears running from the corners of her pinched eyes and her entire body aching as if she'd been flung from a great height to lie here spread-eagled and powerless on her back trusting to a giant of a black man not to smash her bones to bits or smother her with his weight and though now he was saying how he loved her *Oh honey oh honey* she felt her consciousness close to extinction seeing overhead the sky lightly fleeced with clouds, layer upon layer of pale clouds, so empty, so without consolation or even the illusion of such, Calla felt her mouth shaping an involuntary smile.
>
> *When had I stopped believing in, what is it—God?*—and Jesus Christ His only begotten son? After loving Tyrell Thompson, or before?

This scene, the last of many between them, immediately precedes their daredevil boat trip, which results in Tyrell's death and a miscarriage for Calla. The scene is high-pitched and Tyrell's roughness reflects the violence that has been done to the couple and that they are about to do to themselves. In looking at the sky and realizing she no longer believes in God, Calla is bound even more tightly to Tyrell and their mad trip down the river.

This scene points again to the need to establish the boundaries and bigotries of the world in which illicit lovers live and thus connect the intensity of the sex scenes between them with their status as outcasts.

SOME LAST WORDS ABOUT THE ILLICIT

Whether your narrator is explicit or elliptical in relating an encounter of forbidden sex, it is up to you to convey the whole complicated picture: who your characters are, where they fit in the culture that forbids sex between them, what kind of culture this is, and what price the characters pay or fear they might pay for their illicit assignations.

11

SOLO SEX:
ALONE, ON THE PHONE,
AND ON THE INTERNET

Since Phil Roth has opened up these fields of athletics I
suppose it will soon be crowded with young and old men
with open flies, beating their wart-colored bones and
squirting various quantities of juice onto the wallpaper. But
candor is, of course, not all that is needed.

—JOHN CHEEVER,
Journals

Women write, men write—at least people identifying
themselves as men and women. I hear from tops, bottoms,
leather freaks, rubber devotees, whip masters, etc. The
letters are intended as lines to inhale or substances to roll
up and smoke. Throwaway intoxicants. Something to make
me come or to make the writer come. New ones arrive as
regularly as pigeons on the sill and the *New York Times* at
the door.

—LAURIE STONE,
"Perverts.com"

In the last six years, the sex act that's undergone what you might call a makeover—a new image, a surge in popularity, and the Presidential Seal of Approval—is the one that is still most difficult to talk about. In some cases, the terms "cybersex" and "phone sex" are now available to describe the inspiration for it, or the excuse for it. The rest of the time we have the usual clinical terms or the usual slang. The popular British slang is "wanking." Less popular, though more poetic, is "playing pocket billiards" (e.g., "He was caught playing pocket billiards"). It has gone from simply being the embarrassing thing you do when you don't have any better offers to being the embarrassing thing you do on the telephone with a lover or a stranger; or with an online chat room partner; or by the light of a lifelike Internet image on the computer screen.

The essential gesture, the physiology, and the psychology haven't changed, but huge pieces of the landscape have.

A common household item in an English family in the late nineteenth century was a German-made *korsette*, a little metal suit of armor fitted over the genitals, used by nervous Victorian parents to keep children from touching themselves. A hundred years later, in 1994, twenty-five years after the publication of Philip Roth's *Portnoy's Complaint*, we were still acutely skittish: the U.S. Surgeon General was fired for remarking that masturbation is a recognized form of human sexuality mentioned in textbooks and should be discussed with high school students. In 1999, the man who fired her came close to losing his own job as president of the United States for lying about having sex (phone and oral) with an intern. A year later, an article by Jane Brody ran in the *New York Times*, declaring that an excessive fondness for cybersex can easily become a full-fledged addiction—and that some 200,000 people in the United States may be afflicted. One psychologist called cybersex "the crack cocaine of sexual compulsivity."

Oh, for the days when this was just a bit of secret pleasure beneath the sheets!

My interest here is in how our changing but still tortured attitudes and our new technology have influenced the fiction we read and write when it involves—playing pocket billiards. As I look over the many literary examples I have gathered—some from the first edition of the book—I see that there are now four separate categories to divide them into, and that useful distinctions about writing might be made about each category: Solo Sex Alone; Solo Sex in Company; Phone Sex; Intimacy on the Internet.

Before turning to the examples, it's worth comparing the ways in which writing about masturbation is different from writing about other kinds of sex.

In its solitary, asocial aspect, it is fundamentally different from the other couples-oriented sexual activities we've examined. A compelling sex scene typically involves an *encounter*, characters in the act of moving toward or away from one another, characters *wanting* to be with each other, struggling and often failing to make connections. Your characters' desires for one another help plots hurtle forward. Conflict between lovers, or between a pair of lovers and the hostile world, can enliven a sex scene with drama and significance. But when the sexual activity is masturbation, typically there is no Other present to play against, no source of potential conflict from among the dramatis personae.

Fantasy is one's partner, and the imagined dialogue is invariably pornographic—intended, that is, to bring one to orgasm. Phone sex and cybersex offer pornographic dialogue and images—as porn movies do—for those who want or need more than their own imaginations can generate. (By contrast, phone sex with a lover, like masturbation in the presence of a lover, can be an expression of trust and intimacy, or, some might say, of another *sort* of trust and intimacy.)

The most famous masturbation passage in literature—not that there is much competition for the prize—belongs to Philip Roth. In a passage typical of the over-the-top tone of *Portnoy's Complaint*, teenage Alex Portnoy admits to some of his fantasies and sex aids.

On an outing of our family association, I once cored an apple, saw to my astonishment (and with the aid of my obsession) what it looked like, and ran off into the woods to fall upon the orifice of the fruit, pretending that the cool and mealy hole was actually between the legs of that mythical being who always called me Big Boy when she pleaded for what no girl in all recorded history had ever had. "Oh shove it in me, Big Boy," cried the cored apple that I banged silly on that picnic. "Big Boy, Big Boy, oh give me all you've got," begged the empty milk bottle that I kept hidden in our storage bin in the basement, to drive wild after school with my vaselined upright. "Come on, Big Boy, come," screamed the maddened piece of liver that, in my own insanity, I bought one afternoon at a butcher shop and, believe it or not, violated behind a billboard on the way to a bar mitzvah lesson.

As sexual activities go, in literature as in life, masturbation has its limitations. And although we may agree, at least sotto voce, that it is the primary sexual activity of mankind, there is no getting around the fact that you usually do it when you don't have any better offers. When you are alone (read: lonely; read: abandoned) or when you feel you might as well be. The plain truth is that it doesn't do anything to help your social life. Alas, it is often a reminder that you don't have one or that there's something missing from the one you have.

Yet it *is* a fact of life, and since the publication of *Portnoy's Complaint* in 1969, it has made frequent appearances in literary fiction. To my mind, the most interesting examples are those that take account of the complicated feelings the activity generates. The character's inner conflict (arousal vs. shame, arousal vs. fear of being caught) can be part or all of the dramatic tension that is important in creating a compelling scene.

As you turn your attention to this subject we are not often asked to consider, look over the general principles in chapters 2 and 3 and see how many you can apply to writing fiction about masturbation. (All of them, I think.) Then add these two suggestions, before turning to the different groups.

1. Don't ignore your uneasy feelings. If writing about masturbation brings up uneasy feelings, you don't have to "cure" yourself of them in order to proceed. As Dorothy Allison has instructed: "Write to your fear." Explore your uncomfortable feelings in the writing. Use them. Exploit them. Bequeath them to your characters. Make a character's shyness, awkwardness, shame, guilt, or fear of getting caught part of the scene.

2. Just write it. You'll have plenty of time to rewrite later— or to learn to live with your embarrassment. In my interview with novelist Joseph Olshan, he spoke a great deal about how "scary" it was for him to write explicitly gay sex scenes in his novel *Nightswimmer.* Though we were speaking generally about the sex scenes in *Nightswimmer,* because it includes a bold and moving masturbation scene, I include some of his comments here:

> I wrote some scenes and I thought, "Oh, my God, I can't believe I wrote this." But I just forced myself to do it. And even now parts of it just make me cringe. . . . I remember a description of when this character finally has anal sex and I thought, "What is my father going to say when he reads this?" At the end of the semester, one of my students said she had read my novel early in the semester and I thought, "Oh, my God, she read that scene!" When you're sitting down to write you have to banish all those thoughts and think: This may go but I need to just do it and get it out. It may be that I don't think it's appropriate ultimately but it's an exercise now. I can see how far I can go, and that's how I do it. But if I really believed it might be published, I think I would find myself having a hard time with it."

GIVEN CIRCUMSTANCES

1. Everyone masturbates. No one wants to talk about it.
2. People are often made uncomfortable reading about it.
3. If you are alone, you don't want to get caught or leave evidence. If you are with others, you generally don't want to be found out by those outside the group.
4. Fantasy typically plays a larger role in masturbation than in partnered sex.
5. It has historically been more openly accepted, expected, discussed, and joked about by males than by females.
6. Masturbation can be a powerful source of solace.
7. It can also be an irrefutable, even if transient, reminder of loneliness, and the shame of loneliness.

SOLO SEX ALONE

In the mid-1990s, three American novels were published that include particularly audacious scenes of characters masturbating. Through sheer force of their boldness and literary authority, they have the effect of challenging us to get over our hang-ups about this activity once and for all.

Susanna Moore's *In the Cut* is a tautly written, erotically charged literary thriller; her prose has the crystalline sharp edges of Joan Didion's. Frannie, a divorced, notably fearless, and sophisticated creative writing teacher, becomes involved with a rough homicide detective after first coming upon him by accident in the basement of a bar, on a couch with, as she says, a woman between his legs. When a Detective Malloy comes to her apartment several days later, canvassing the neighborhood as he investigates a murder, Frannie does not recognize him immediately. It seems a part of the murdered woman's body was found in Washington Square Park, across the street from her building. Had Frannie heard anything unusual that night? So begins an electrifying dance between these two strong-willed, sexually adventurous characters.

Frannie describes their several sexual encounters with a full-throttle, pornographic intensity; she wants us to feel the power of what turns out to be her dangerous attraction to Malloy. His first visit is business laced only with flirtation, but sleeping alone after he leaves, she dreams about him, and when she masturbates early the next morning, he is her fantasy:

I pushed aside my pillows and turned onto my stomach. My feet hung off the end of the bed, my toes hooked over the edge. The way I do. And through my cotton nightgown, I put two fingers of my right hand on my clitoris and thought of him. Standing in a room, coming toward me, watching me undress. . . . (It must always be through a nightgown or a pair of underpants. I've wondered if this is because of the greater friction. Surely that must be part of it, but there is something more, perhaps the thrill that first came to me as a small girl, pressing my fingers against myself, the cloth interceding between my fingers and my vagina, interceding between shame and pleasure). . . .

One Sunday morning in boarding school I found my room-mate lying on her back on the tile floor of the shower stall. Her legs . . . were splayed on either side of the spigots, the water cascading between her slack muscular thighs. . . . She remains to this day the only woman I've ever known who spoke freely of her own masturbation. She urged me to try it. I didn't have the courage to tell her that I had found my own way. Women will talk about anything—sexual jealousy, dishonor, the lovely advantages of eating pussy or sucking cock—but they will not tell you about fucking themselves.

So there was Detective Malloy, watching me take off my clothes.

My clitoris swelled under my fingers. . . . It is not the same as when a man's fingers are there. . . . I am confident when it is my hand. Sometimes . . . I get a terrible cramp in my calf and I have to leap up and limp around the room until it goes away.

Malloy was happy to wait.

This brief passage is an entire social history on the subject of women and masturbation in our culture, a history of silence and shame. The power of the writing is in Frannie's directness, specificity, and honesty about the tension between physical pleasure and secret shame. The movement in the passage is from Frannie's physical experience in her childhood memory to a boarding school memory when she is older, to the adult's knowledge of the greater world of women and how rare the boarding school experience was, and then back to the specific moment in which she is fantasizing that Malloy is watching her. We are meant to imagine that while masturbating, Frannie journeys back in time and deep into her psyche; the return to Malloy watching is a kind of comfort, a relief from the pull of memories and feelings of shame. Malloy watching is an endorsement of what she is doing; in fact, in one of their sex scenes later in the novel, Malloy *does* watch while she touches herself.

By contrast, there *is* a well-traveled place in the culture for boys and men to talk about masturbation, joke about it, even, as teenagers, engage in it together, and, since Philip Roth, for male writers to write comically about it. The gesture of a male masturbating is a vulgar commonplace, something kids do behind other kids' backs; something we have seen in the movies, if we haven't in real life. There's a vivid scene in Federico Fellini's autobiographical film *Amarcord*, in which a group of horny, rowdy teenage boys sets a car rocking and makes its headlights blink in something meant to resemble orgasmic excitement.

It is the knowing male culture of masturbation that Rick Moody has so much fun with in the satiric opening chapter of *The Ice Storm*, as middle-aged, married Benjamin Hood waits for his mistress to return to the bed in her guest room, in the suburban house where, in the year 1973, she, her husband, and kids live down the road from Ben, his wife, and their kids. When she does not return to the room, Hood wanders around her well-appointed house. When he enters her teenage son's room, he notes the hippie drug-culture decorating scheme and imagines pornographic magazines between the mattresses

with socks crusty with his dried seed. The shame and resource-fulness of the masturbator coming into his craft! . . . Mike's laundry was probably welded together with his semen.

Imagine the sheer volume of it at single-sex schools and in penitentiaries. Consider how often the average American male masturbated in 1973. That year there were, say, 100 million American men, two-thirds of whom were capable of achieving orgasm. At once a week that meant approximately 3,432,000,000 ejaculations in the calendar year. . . .

[Hood] had tried to explain self-abuse to his son once, and this was one of the conversations that did not go well. He sat the boy down in the bedroom one day and asked him not to do it in the shower, because it wasted water and electricity and because everyone would expect it of him there anyway, and not to do it onto the linen, and not to do it with his sister's under-garments or any clothes belonging to his mother, and not to do it with the dog. The best time was when he was certain no one else was in the house. The best place was in the john, where it would cause no trouble and mix with the other sad waste prod-ucts of America. If he became concerned about any sign of per-version in his habits, he should feel free to come forward and discuss it. Together they could consult a medical text.

At the close of this monologue, [his son] looked as though he had just learned of his family's financial ruin.

A few pages later Hood himself, with no sign of his mistress anywhere, masturbates into her discarded garter belt and, desperate for someplace to hide it, shoves it into the back of the teenage son's closet. All of these gestures will weave their way through the intricate plot and come back to haunt these interconnected households.

The boisterous, comic tone of the excerpt could not be more different from Susanna Moore's. The emotional power of Moore's scene arises partly from the riskiness of a woman discussing it so bluntly in the first place; the power of Moody's partly from the father's twisted notion that this instructional monologue is his idea of closeness between father and son. But even before the monologue, the father's fixation on masturbation—he doesn't even see the teenage boy's magazines, he just imagines that they are there—and his leap to macro-male thinking about it—number of men, ejaculations per year—reveal that men and women have vastly different relationships to the subject.

The writing in the two examples has many common elements. It is specific to the characters, voice, and tone of the books. The masturbation scenes in both introduce plot devices or foreshadow other sex scenes. For Frannie, the scene conveys to us more dramatically than any exposition could that she is attracted to Malloy; her attraction will be her undoing. But what the two examples share most is a fierce gutsiness.

The third example, from Philip Roth's *Sabbath's Theater,* is pure Rothian excess, a possible snapshot of Portnoy at sixty-four, masturbating on the grave of his married lover Drenka, who died of cancer at fifty-two, only five months before. They had a combative, baroque, sexually adventurous sex life for thirteen years; each was married and had lovers. The novel opens with Drenka, still alive, insisting that he stop sleeping with other women and him refusing—though we soon learn that, at this point, he is only *pretending* to sleep with other women. Six months later, she is dead and Sabbath is bereft.

He visits her grave on many nights. Now that she's dead, of course, he wants to marry her.

"So now you want me all to yourself. Now," she said, "when you don't have to have only men and live only with me and be bored only by me, now I am good enough to be your wife."

"Marry me!"

Smiling invitingly, she replied, "First you'll have to die," and raised Silvija's dress to reveal that she was without underpants—dark stockings and a garter belt but no underpants. Even dead, Drenka gave him a hard-on; alive *or* dead. Drenka made him twenty again. Even with the temperatures below zero, he would grow hard whenever, from her coffin, she enticed him like this. He had learned to stand with his back to the north so that the icy wind did not blow directly on his dick but still he had to remove one of his gloves to jerk off successfully, and sometimes the gloveless hand would get so cold that he would have to put the glove back on and switch to the other hand. He came on her grave many nights.

ALONE AND TOGETHER

Often in fiction—and masturbation, too—the more the merrier. When an author moves this most solitary of activities into a group setting, possibilities for drama, conflict, character development, and plot follow right along. A character alone can have an interesting interior life, but two characters together can make sparks fly, whether they're making love, masturbating, or solving a murder. In the Alice Lukens example below, a group of fifth-grade girls, who masturbate on gym ropes and as a result call themselves the Vine Sisters, add a new twist to female bonding. And in the excerpts from *Bastard Out of Carolina*, Ruth Anne's tacit understanding with her sister about their common activity, which they sometimes practice while sleeping in the same bed, allows them a glancing closeness that nothing else in their relationship permits.

Ruth Anne Boatwright, narrator of *Bastard Out of Carolina*, Dorothy Allison's powerful novel of incest and family violence, is as blunt in expressing her feelings on masturbation as she is in everything else. As a girl Ruth Anne is raped and repeatedly beaten by her stepfather, Daddy Glen, as her mother listens on the other side of a door, washes the girl's face afterward, and urges her "not to be so stubborn, not to make him mad." When Ruth Anne begins to masturbate, in the bedroom she shares with her sister, she fantasizes people watching Daddy Glen beat her, creating a tortured connection between the violence done to her and the pleasure she wants to give herself. She narrates using language that combines the child's terror and longing with the adult's more cool-eyed understanding of the complex dynamics far beyond a child's comprehension:

> When he beat me, I screamed and kicked and cried like the baby I was: But sometimes when I was safe and alone, I would imagine the ones who watched. Someone had to watch—some girl I admired who barely knew I existed, some girl from church or down the street. . . . In my imagination I was proud and defiant. I'd stare back at him with my teeth set, making no sound at all, no shameful scream, no begging. Those who watched admired me and hated him. I pictured it that way and put my hands between my legs. It was scary, but it was thrilling too. Those who watched me, loved me. It was as if I was being beaten for them. I was wonderful in their eyes. . . .
> I was ashamed of myself for the things I thought about when I put my hands between my legs, more ashamed for masturbating to the fantasy of being beaten than for being beaten in the first place. I lived in a world of shame. I hid my bruises as if they were evidence of crimes I had committed. I knew I was a sick and disgusting person. I couldn't stop my stepfather from beating me, but *I* was the one who masturbated. *I* did that, and how could I explain to anyone that I hated being beaten but still masturbated to the story I told myself about it?
> Yet . . . I loved those fantasies, even though I was sure they were a terrible thing. They had to be; they were self-centered

and they made me have shuddering orgasms. In them, I was very special. I was triumphant, important. I was not ashamed. There was no heroism possible in the real beatings. There was just being beaten until I was covered with snot and misery.

Later in the novel, Ruth Anne discovers her sister is also masturbating often, sometimes while they are in the bed they share at night. When they return from school in the afternoons, they have a tacit agreement to give each other time alone in the bedroom. One afternoon, Ruth Anne walks in on her sister and finds her with a pair of their mother's underpants covering her face. In their conspiracy of silence and shame, Ruth Anne grabs a book she had been reading and pretends not to have seen anything. During this period the sisters barely speak to each other, "but we made sure no one else ever went in the bedroom when one of us was there alone."

Allison's emphasis throughout is *not* on the details of stimulation; the narrative does not lead toward the orgasm. How could it? The pleasurable physical sensations are so tainted and twisted by Ruth Anne's memories and disturbing fantasies that masturbating is a kind of self-inflicted punishment that she nevertheless cannot stop doing. The narrative moves instead toward insight and illumination, to an understanding of what these events and moments felt like to Ruth Anne as a child and how she makes sense of them now looking back.

Ruth Anne is as candid when writing about masturbation as she is when relating her stepfather's brutality or her mother's divided loyalties; she makes no attempts to prettify, to gloss over humiliations, to make her characters look better than they are.

In the scene with the sister, Allison explores one of the given circumstances of masturbation: we don't want to be found out. The sisters are found out by each other, but the furtive nature of the act means there will not be a confrontation. The passages are especially moving because they hint at a loyalty and intimacy between the girls that is not expressed or acknowledged otherwise. Their unspoken secret seems to be the only basis for any closeness between them.

• These scenes remind us that masturbation scenes, like all good sex scenes, cannot be plunked down in the middle of a story either to titillate or take up space. They must be stitched in, so they connect to the larger concerns of the work.

If masturbation is fraught with anguish and guilt for Ruth Anne Boatwright, in the very different universe of Alice Lukens it is a source of female bonding, group giggles, and only fleeting embarrassment. These passages from *The Vine Sisters* are from a collection of short stories Lukens wrote for her senior thesis in creative writing at Princeton University in 1995. These are the only scenes I have come across in which female characters acknowledge and celebrate group masturbation.

In this scene from a story also called "The Vine Sisters," narrator Kate describes what happens after lunch at her girls' private school:

Sometimes, to goof off, we swung from vine to vine like Tarzan and Jane. We hung upside down from the branches and did flips, our uniform skirts falling down around our faces. Our shirts came untucked and our socks fell down around our ankles and nobody was there to yell at us or give us detentions for it. But mostly, we went to get It.

I first discovered It in first grade one day, climbing a pole. I got It climbing trees and ropes and rocks, rubbing against an old wooden horse in the playground, shimmying up swingset poles, rubbing against doors at home, my bedpost, my bureau, my pillows, my stuffed animals. Kay could get It by just crossing and uncrossing her legs. I couldn't get It that way, or only a little bit, not like on a rope. Kay said she saw her older sister crossing and uncrossing her legs sometimes in the kitchen when she didn't know Kay was looking. Diana, Beth, and I didn't have sisters, just brothers. But both Diana and Beth, like me, said they had known about It a long time, for as long as they could remember.

We discovered each other in gym classes in fourth grade, climbing ropes. I wouldn't let myself feel It until the very top, not until I touched the ceiling. Then I would let myself sit there for a little while, just hanging and feeling It between my legs and looking down on everyone on the gym floor. I noticed when Diana and Kay climbed they would do the same thing, shimmy way up the rope and then just hang there, moving their legs a little bit, looking down at everybody. That's how I knew. We were the only three who could climb all the way up the rope and touch the ceiling. . . .

We called ourselves the Vine Sisters. We had two membership requirements: It, and secrecy. Sometimes in the middle of class somebody would say "it," talking about something entirely different, and we would look at each other and laugh and think *if only they knew.* Sometimes even thinking about it was enough to make It do a somersault or two between our legs.

A year later, in fifth grade, Kate notices a new shy girl on the ropes who also seems to have It, and she and a few other Vine Sisters try to "recruit a new member, Cary." They led her to the bathroom for a grilling:

> "We want to ask you a question," said Kay.
> "Okay," Cary said.
> "When you climb ropes," I blurted, "do you feel something between your legs?"
> "We all do," said Beth, "so don't worry if you do."

Cary surprised us all and started to cry.

"Don't cry!" Kay cried out. "We all feel it! It's wonderful! We have a club. We call ourselves the Vine Sisters and—"

The door to the bathroom swung open, and Ms. Richter, our math teacher, entered. We hushed up and grinned.

Cary runs from them and the Vine Sisters confer, wishing "she weren't so ashamed," but deciding that she probably won't get them into trouble because "she's so embarrassed she can't even talk to us." They decide to quit their recruiting efforts and maintain the secret society.

Though the Vine Sisters are not embarrassed by what they do in one another's presence, they know that It is taboo, and It must be kept a secret. The author uses the secret status of the group to create enough dramatic tension to move the story forward and sow conflict between characters (the group and Cary, the group and Ms. Richter).

The most engaging surprise to me in these passages is the narrator's breezy openness on the subject. She is atypically plucky, unabashed, and seemingly without shame or embarrassment in her pursuits of It. And the fact that It is not just her own private pleasure but a conspiracy of pleasure, a private club that, CIA-like, operates furtively in public, creates ripples of literary pleasure for the reader.

PHONE SEX

Nicholson Baker's best-selling 1992 novel, *Vox*, put phone sex on the literary map. A transcript of a single phone-sex conversation between strangers, this brief novel surprised readers with its pornographic explicitness, and, I think, because the characters went on for 161 pages at exorbitant phone-sex rates about the minutiae of their sexual pasts, particularly as they related to masturbation. The man and woman were not exactly strangers by the time they finally had their simultaneous orgasms, complete with verbal soundtrack. The novel's last line, "They hung up," says as much about the insular world of the book and its emotional terrain as the opening line: "'What are you wearing?' he asked."

The excerpt below from Joseph Olshan's *Nightswimmer*, a mournful and romantic novel about gay New York in the 1990s, makes phone sex an incident in the character's life, rather than his entire fictional identity. It also introduces another element of our telephone lives, Call Waiting, which, had it been widely available when Baker wrote *Vox*, might have enlarged his canvas considerably.

In this scene from *Nightswimmer*, Will, the main character, has called a telephone sex line where he speaks at length to his "phone-sex partner," and begins to masturbate, coming close to orgasm, when he is interrupted by Call Waiting. He takes the call, hoping it is his new lover, and finds instead the jealous friend, Peter, who introduced Will to the new lover. After exchanging some sharp words, Will clicks off, intending to call back the phone-sex line. But there is no need to; Will finds the man still on the line, courtesy of Call Waiting:

> I'd already forgotten his name. Not that it mattered, because he'd probably given me a phony name anyway.
> "Wow!" I said, "you waited." I felt an amazing tenderness for this disembodied voice who probably lied about the way he looked, but who was obviously patient, maybe even steadfast. Suddenly I thought I could feel his loneliness there in the outlying borough that bordered La Guardia Airport and Flushing Bay, a residential area dismissed by the Manhattan elite as being declassé. And it occurred to me, as I began urging myself and this guy toward a late-night climax, that perhaps I could persuade him to become my monogamous phone lover.

What *happens* in this scene is that Will masturbates on the telephone with a stranger, but what the scene is *about* is the power of loneliness to draw people together.

Here again, Olshan's emphasis is not on the progress of the orgasm but on the mood, the emotional and cultural ambience, the far-reaching loneliness of the big city, the disembodied voices, the tiny lies we tell each other in order to connect across these chasms. The paragraph ends with a wonderful, haunting irony: you could be faithful to the disembodied voice of a stranger on your telephone. Instead of a masturbation fantasy that summons a person, this dreamer yearns only for a loyal voice on the phone—perhaps the ideal sex partner in the age of AIDS.

INTIMACY ON THE INTERNET

Phone sex is a straightforward endeavor. Even if it is beyond one's experience or appetite, it is not difficult to describe in words or to depict dramatically. (Baker told his story entirely in dialogue; Olshan integrated his scene into the narrative of the story.) The same cannot be said about the vast, otherworldly subject of cybersex, which involves a range of physical and cerebral activities more suited to science fiction than the kind of fiction we have been examining up to now. The sexual stimulation available to almost anyone with a computer and a modem now includes porn sites; erotic webzines, such as nerve.com; chat rooms; and e-mail communications with strangers and friends, whom we may or may not have met in the flesh.

But despite these far-flung destinations, these worlds within worlds and worlds beyond worlds, what we're really talking about when we talk about an individual having cybersex or "sex on the Internet" is masturbation with hardware. Whether someone is visiting a site called bigtits.com or carrying on a torrid all-night correspondence with a lover in Juno, Alaska, the flesh-and-blood humans are confined to sitting or reclining in front of computer screens, with, as they say, one hand on the keyboard.

Given the popularity of these activities in real life, I set out to discover how they have filtered down into the fiction we write and read at the turn of the millennium—and what sort of literary guidance I might offer writers who have been lured in this direction. (Please note, I am not referring here to fiction with sexual content that appears on Internet sites and webzines. My interest is in fiction that involves characters who connect via e-mail or the Internet; fiction in which the computer and the Net are elements in the story.)

My curiosity has taken me to places I hadn't anticipated, and has brought to mind Anthony Burgess's comment, "I am not inclined to fault those who look for sex in literature; looking for sex, they may find something else."

The novels and short stories I read are as varied and difficult to summarize as the Internet itself. Without shelves of established fiction to choose from, I solicited suggestions from friends and colleagues, combed nerve.com's website, read a well-known hypertext novel on CD-ROM, *Patchwork Girl,* by Shelley Jackson, and read a pile of novels printed on paper that had Internet-related titles or that seemed, from reviews I read, to explore relationships forged or abetted by e-mail connections. I didn't know ahead of time how much sex I would encounter—and sometimes wasn't sure afterward how much I had encountered. With the technical intricacies of *Patchwork Girl,* I wasn't sure I had even found the entire novel. Once I finished reading everything, I was baffled for weeks about what lessons I might draw for this chapter—until I realized that there might be no lessons as I understood them elsewhere in the book.

The lesson, I began to see, is that everything is up for grabs.

Choosing a starting place for this discussion bears some resemblance to the experience of surfing the World Wide Web: beginnings, middles, and ends don't have the same weight they do on dry land. Hierarchies don't either: you can cover the territory regardless of where you start. The truth is an ever-shifting mosaic, not a slab of concrete.

One place to begin is with the obvious, essential question: How do fiction writers integrate the hardware (computer), the software (browser, Internet service provider, operating system), and the humanware (emotions, relationships)?

There are still a few bugs in the system, but writers are inventive, and each has tackled the problem differently. Some have taken the technical complexities by the horns. Others have figured out ways to avoid them altogether.

These six very different examples suggest some of the possibilities and pitfalls in writing fiction about intimacy on the Internet.

THE E-MAIL NOVEL

English writer Matt Beaumont's *e: A Novel,* is a fast-paced farce told entirely in e-mail, published in 2000. It's great fun to read, with the manic, high-energy humor of two other English productions, *Monty Python's Flying Circus* and Michael Frayn's play *Noises Off.*

The setting is a trendy London advertising agency with branches around the world; in one recurring gag, the boss's e-mail keeps inadvertently being sent to the Helsinki office and his efforts to get it fixed repeatedly fail. The characters range from the senior executive to a cleaning woman still learning English who sneaks some computer time to send an e-mail to her distant son. The central drama revolves around the company's efforts to win the Coca-Cola account. What threatens their success are their own foibles, jealousies, pettiness, laziness, and office romances spinning out of control, not to mention the sheer volume of e-mail they transmit in the course of a day, through which all of these dramas are narrated.

Though the sexual content of *e* is slender, it does a wonderful job depicting the brave new world of forthright sexual communication we have entered. Coyness and flirtation have gone the way of the rotary telephone. E-mail invites a directness and candor—at least sexual candor—that isn't always as easy to express when people are face to face. And the abundance of pornographic language that we're exposed to on the Internet, even as passive recipients of unsolicited e-mail, has rippled through all of our speech and changed the standards for casual chat.

The passages below from *e* are references to sex, not summaries and not enactments, but they have a haikulike charm and are entirely appropriate both to the office setting and the e-mail medium, which leaves no time for leisurely seductions. These are cut-to-the-chase propositions. This is life lived in e-mail time: "See you in thirty seconds," one lover writes to another.

Nigel, the fussy office manager–type in the accounts department, sends an officewide e-mail with a P.S.: "On my return I found some lady's underthings by the lift door in reception. They're size 12, emerald green, 100% polyester with a lacy panel at the front, slightly soiled. If they belong to anyone, they're tucked safely in my drawer. Please feel free to collect."

Ten pages later, Liam O'Keefe sends Lorraine Pallister an e-mail titled, "Re: knickers, emerald green, medium," with this message: "If I can discreetly retrieve them from accounts, fancy losing them again tonight?"

Liam then sends an e-mail to Nigel, "re: Victoria's Secret." The message: "Nige, discretion on this is appreciated, but the scanties in your drawer are mine. Pop them in a brown bag and hand them over when we have a beer. When are you free? Tonight? Can't wait, pal."

Later:

From: Liam O'Keefe
To: Lorraine Pallister
Re: Joy of Sex, pp 13, 48, 97, 122

I'm horny. What are you doing tonight?

When Lorraine explains she has other plans, he immediately e-mails another woman in the office, but his solicitation is more restrained:

To: Katie Philplott
Re: plans

Tonight?

Later still, Lorraine writes:

To: Liam O'Keefe
Re: busy?

On my way in this morning I found out how to make the lift stop between floors. When are you free for elevator maintenance?

His answer: "I've got a snapper to brief, ten press ads to draw up and accounts are screaming for my time sheets . . . see you in thirty seconds."

It's uncertain whether we'll see more novels told entirely in e-mail, but Beaumont's effort demonstrates that there are more possibilities for incorporating sex into Internet-specific fiction than our narrow definitions of cybersex had suggested.

OTHER INTERNET FICTION

The novel written in e-mail puts us at the computer screen with the other characters; we see what they see. Actually, we see more, because we see everyone's e-mail. By contrast, in the other works of fiction I've looked at, computer communications are mediated through a character or two. Instead of seeing their computer screen exclusively, we see the screen through their eyes and their psyches. We are given explanations of the mechanics of their Internet lives; meditations on the nature of this alternate world; conversations between them and other characters who do and don't understand their obsessions; and samples, oftentimes extended, of their e-mail correspondence.

We might say that writers handle these awkward challenges with varying degrees of grace, or that the omnipresence of this new equipment and these new universes has forced us to redefine grace.

One of the earliest examples of a character engaged in cybersex appears in David Leavitt's 1989 novel, *Equal Affections.* Walter, who lives with Danny in a suburb of New York City, becomes increasingly involved with the world of online gay sex. He eventually has an online partner, whom he also talks to on the telephone. Because these worlds were so new to us in the mid- and late-1980s, when the book was written, Leavitt takes particular care to explain and explore the physical and psychic territory in ways that are straightforward and psychologically astute.

Although the impetus for these connections is sexual, the cybersex in *Equal Affections* happens almost in parentheses. The narrative and the dramatic tension involving the Internet focus on the complicated, perplexing nature of Walter's fixation on this new medium, not on any details of masturbation.

In his New York City office after hours, Walter sits down at his computer, presses a few buttons, types a few codes, and enters a chat room whose participants are named Hot Leather, Teen Slave Master, and NY Jock:

> This endless conversation, to which he might always gain access, was the closest Walter came these days to actually cheating on Danny. He'd join in the dialogue, the circle of talk, and sometimes a message would appear, "Please talk with NY Jock.

To do so, enter/TALK 125." Once it had gotten so frantic they had switched to the phone. Their voices caressed each other; they pretended their own hands were each other's hands. Afterwards, half naked, spent, Walter slumped in his chair, looking out the window at the skyline. . . . He didn't give out his own number or his last name. What drew him to this game was the very fact of its anonymity.

Later, when Walter connects with a man whose screen name is Bulstrode, Bulstrode describes to him his Internet love life, shocking Walter with what is now commonplace: that people can develop deep attachments, even fall in love, with people they have never met. Bulstrode's most serious gay relationship was with such a man; and the sex was great, he tells Walter.

> "You mean phone sex?" Walter said cautiously.
> "Yes, of course. The most intense, incredible, horny, hot phone sex I have ever had. Sometimes we'd be on the phone five, six hours. He always came three or four times, but I held back. I wanted to wait until the very end and then really make it big."
> "You always like to wait a long time before you come?"
> "I sure do. How about you?"
> Their conversation took a different direction. Afterwards, sweaty and spent, Walter crawled into bed next to Danny, who lay rigid, facing the wall.
> "Have fun with your boys?" Danny said.
> "Sure," Walter said. He tried to laugh at what had just happened to him, turn it into a joke, a light diversion, as Danny imagined it was, but all that night, Walter couldn't get Bulstrode out of his mind. There was something irresistible about him, about the very noncorporeality of him, as if he really were that imaginary friend most children invent at some moment or another.

The appeal of the Internet was novel and newsworthy in *Equal Affections*. By the time Jeanette Winterson's novel *The Powerbook* appeared, appropriately in 2000, we needed fewer explanations for the intoxicating power of the new medium. In fact, without the reader's prior knowledge of the computer and its allure, the book would be incomprehensible, instead of intriguing and deliciously ambiguous. The chapter titles are computer allusions—OPEN HARD DRIVE, SEARCH, VIEW, EMPTY TRASH, SHOW BALLOONS—and the narrator begins sitting at her computer, opening an e-mail that invites "Freedom, just for one night." The freedom to be somebody else.

In *The Powerbook,* as in much of Winterson's work, boundaries blur, characters move between centuries, historic figures appear in times and places in which they never lived, and we return again and again to the quotidian terrain of longing and love, mostly unrequited, in the late twentieth century. What Winterson adds to the mix here is an Internet Age premise: these two e-mail correspondents are inventing the identities and stories they will tell that night.

> There was a pause—then I tapped out, "Let's start. What color hair do you want?"
>
> "Red. I've always wanted red hair. . . . So what shall I wear?"
>
> "It's up to you. Combat or Prada?"
>
> "How much can I spend on clothes?"
>
> "How about $1000?"
>
> "My whole wardrobe or just one outfit?"
>
> "Are you doing this story on a budget?"
>
> "You're the writer."
>
> "It's your story."
>
> "What happened to the omniscient author?"
>
> "Gone interactive."
>
> "Look . . . I know this was my idea, but maybe we should quit."

"What's the problem? This is art not telephone sex."

"I know, and I said I wanted the freedom to be somebody else—just for one night . . ."

"We've started. We're here."

"But where are we?"

"You tell me . . ."

"Paris. We're in Paris. There's the Eiffel Tower."

The next chapter, called NEW DOCUMENT, is a seemingly straightforward narrative of two women walking along the banks of the Seine who have recently met. In a hotel room soon after— though time is hard to tell in this doubly invented encounter— the women become lovers.

This is how we made love.

You kissed my throat.

The boy was dancing.

You kissed my collarbone.

Two taxi drivers were arguing in the street.

You put your tongue into the channel of my breasts.

A door slammed underneath us.

I opened your legs onto my hip.

Two pigeons were asleep under the red wings of the roof.

You began to move with me—hands, tongue, body.

Game-show laughter from the television next door.

You took my breasts in both hands and I slid you out of your jeans.

Rattle of bottles on a tray.

You don't wear knickers.

A door opened. The tray was set down.

You keep your breasts in a black mesh cage.

Car headlights reflected in the dressing-table mirror.

Lie down with me.

Get on top of me.

Ease yourself, just there, just there . . .
Harry speaks French, he'll pick up the beer.
Push.
Stella or Bud?
Harder.
Do you want nuts?
Make me come. Make me.
Ring her after midnight your time, she said.
Just fuck me.
Got the number?
Fuck me.

Subscribing to traditional gender roles, some of the gay men in *Equal Affections* want heavy doses of anonymous telephone and chat room sex. By contrast, the women in *The Powerbook* begin their invented lives choosing a designer wardrobe and a real city known for romance. When it comes to the earthbound matter of sex, the writer delivers, not a lonely masturbator at the computer, but a poetic, mock-traditional sex scene, layered with tenderness, unlikely juxtapositions, and incipient orgasms.

The magic of *The Powerbook* is that the writer/narrator is creating the story she tells and transmitting it to her e-mail partner, but as we read the story invented for the occasion, we come to believe it's something other than words on the computer screen. It's sparely written, intensely immediate, and includes no reminders of hardware or Internet providers. It meets the test: it feels as "real" as any story we read in a novel.

Kit Reed's novel *@expectations,* published in 2000, is the most conceptually adventurous of the Internet fiction I've found. It's *Madame Bovary* with a high-speed modem and a taste for science fiction. An unhappily married woman, Jenny Wilder, finds a baroque Internet community called StElene, with its own Grand-

Hotel, and a collection of characters with elaborate histories and histrionics. She becomes addicted to the site, falls in love with a man whose screen name is Reverdy, as in reverie, and eventually pursues the real-life man to Alaska. But before all of that, Reed immerses us in the complex goings on at StElene, where characters occasionally have cybersex in passing, without much angst or explanation: "Then last night on StElene [Vinnie and Mireya] were making love online, so easy, so often, so sexy, so safe."

What is most interesting to me in *@expectations* is not the sex—there isn't much—but the reach of Reed's inventions and her characters' inner and outer conflicts about their online lives:

> Most lovers shower before they get back into bed with the injured party, but like so much that Jenny is invested in, this love is ephemeral. Nothing. In material terms, she and Reverdy have done nothing. And yet.
>
> The flush at her throat, the aura are too pervasive to be erased by scrubbing. Physical love you finish and forget, but what Jenny has with Reverdy grows in the imagination. It fills rooms. No. The words that they exchange faster than thought—what they say and do, the expectation of what they will say and do next time and the anticipation—are lyric. Their love is tremendous.

The only person who knows about Jenny's online life is her friend Margaret, who is blunt with her:

> "This is sick, Jenny. How did you get so tied up in something you can't see? You think you're in a movie or something? Or is it more like a game? Are we talking imaginary playmates, or what?"
>
> "It's as real as you and me sitting here."
>
> She shakes her head. "It's all typing in the dark to me."

"We type, and things *exist*. . . . Do you have any idea what it's like to get to the level of pure thought? StElene is like that; people getting past the superficial, meeting on the plane of pure thought."

The punch line to the book is that life on StElene is as full of impurity and imperfection as life everywhere else. What trips people up in real *and* imagined worlds are not the mechanics of sex or even the limitations of cybersex, but the unbearable weight of longing, our immense need to make connections—and our ordinary human failure to make them last.

Two final examples are short stories specifically about Internet sex. William Burkett Jr.'s "Addiction," published in an anthology, *Aqua Erotica* (Three Rivers Press and Melcher Media Dura-Books), is a straightforward story about a man communicating—and having "sex" with his online lover, D, as he sits in a cafe, wearing a special chip in his eyeglasses that keeps others from being able to see his screen. Early on, he reveals his reasons for this kind of love affair: "The magic of the computer age: intimate contact across a continent, or ocean. Swift rapport, almost telepathic in its intensity. No risk of disease, no messy exchange of body fluids, no risk at all. Except heartbreak."

He also reveals that he has a piece of illegal software that allows him to view D's online life, and that she has many cyber-dalliances, not to mention a real-life husband. Before long, still sitting in the cafe, he and D drift into a heated cyber-romp, complete with porno soundtrack and what sounds like simultaneous orgasms. While he stops short of disrobing or unsheathing, he tells us, "I can feel her now—truly feel her—so that my hips roll on the coffee-shop chair as if thrusting up. I can feel my testicles draw up, tight, and a shadow of the old hard ache of real-life lust floods me." Afterward, "Every passerby must have known what I was doing."

Moments later, the narrator finds D back with her other online lovers and he, too, we learn, has a distant girlfriend into whose open cyber-arms he takes shelter and comfort. The story ends with him ordering another cup of coffee and typing.

In Laurie Stone's much more substantial story, "Perverts.com," (available in the fiction archives at nerve.com and in a paperback collection, *Full Frontal Fiction: The Best of nerve.com*), the narrator, in journalistic fashion, introduces us to the world of online "perverts" and takes us through twenty pages of cyber-relationships, the majority of the text taken up with her eaves-dropping on, and becoming aroused by, chatty and pornographic e-mails that go between other members of the website/chat room "Fetishes R Us." The names of some of the sites she mentions in passing are funny—or maybe only to those of us who haven't spent time on porn websites: fuckmeharder.com, oneblonde fingeringanother.com, pregnantandlactatingsluts.com, sodatbitch ruinedyourlife.com.

What isn't funny is the loneliness that runs through the story. So much, in this addictive world, depends upon the fix, the response to the e-mail that doesn't come. The narrator eventually "opens up" and writes to "scratchandsniff and everydayfiend," whose letters have stopped showing up in the system:

> I am saddened by your absence and wish you would return, for I have greatly enjoyed your revelations. You give flesh and personality to horniness. How many times have I masturbated in the arms of a blank? No name. No face, sometimes. Often, no words.

But when her letter is not answered, she tells us that she "sought consolation in the flesh. . . . What is it about the thoughts that are summoned, the pulsing of the body, the going out for those moments of bliss until the shudders subside and you return to the place you left, no better no worse, though feeling peculiarly detached from the desire that only minutes before seemed so urgent. . . .?"

This narrator ends the story still in the grip of her own obsession—with the sex lives of others.

These varied works of fiction don't point resoundingly in a single direction on the matter of writing about Internet intimacy, except perhaps to reaffirm its limitations—and suggest how some writers have managed to subvert the limitations. Sex scenes in Beaumont's *e* take place offstage; e-mail is the medium for lovers to proposition each other and take care of business: retrieving stray underpants and the like. For Jeanette Winterson, e-mail is not a sex aide but a muse—or easy access to a muse.

As we become more accustomed to the role of the Internet in our lives, it's not at all clear that droves of fiction writers will be flocking to this arena, now that the initial novelty has faded.

But for writers who do go there, this fast-changing fantasy world is an erotic retreat, a vast space where we can try to redefine love, loyalty, intimacy, and, of course, sex. We can tailor them to suit us, to please us, to pleasure us—but fortunately for fiction writers, when we venture into cyberspace, we venture as humans, not microchips. We go with our fingers, our screen names—and our hearts, which even in cyberspace can be easily broken. We go full of yearning, full of desire, and we don't always get what we want. So much the better for writers of fiction. Online and off, in the worlds of high-tech software and flesh and blood, a character who wants something, who pursues what she wants and keeps being thwarted in her efforts, is a character we can care about, and the heart of a compelling piece of fiction.

EXERCISES

1. "I could never tell anyone _____" (fill in the blank). This is an exercise Dorothy Allison routinely gives her students. The blank does not have to have anything to do with sex. It also does not need to be true.

2. **Given Circumstances.** Chapters 5 through 11 focus on specific sexual relationships—between first-time lovers, married people, adulterers, etc.—and what they mean for the fiction writer. Here are five other possible sexual relationships. For each one, write a list of given circumstances (characteristics that are true in every or almost every case) and comb your memory for examples from novels or short stories. Consult the examples you remembered and see how many of your given circumstances apply:

   a. Sex partners for the purposes of conception
   b. Sex partners for hire
   c. Sex between partners of very different ages
   d. Sex between people who were lovers when they were much younger, have been separated, and are meeting again in old age

e. Sex between people who were once a couple but are no longer

3. **Write your own.** The best sex scenes arise from the needs, histories, and compulsions of your characters. But for practice purposes, write a few freestanding sex scenes and see what you come up with. Begin with the types of sexual relationships listed above. For each type of relationship, write two scenes, one intended to be funny and one not funny. Include well-defined, clearly motivated characters, plenty of details, at least a little conflict, a few surprises, and dialogue where necessary.

4. **Explicit vs. Discreet.** Experiment with the sex scenes you have written above. First, make them more sexually explicit than they are now, then less explicit. Look at all the versions a week later and see what works and what doesn't work as well. Look again a month later. Have your perceptions and judgments changed?

5. **Talk to me.** Write a sex scene using only dialogue. We should come to the end of the scene knowing who the characters are, what they want or wanted from the encounter, what they want in a broader sense, and whether they have gotten what they wanted. The dialogue should also reveal where the scene is taking place: what part of the world, what room, etc.

6. **Location, location, location.** Write a sex scene in which the sense of place is central to the encounter. Sense of place = country, city, actual spot (the room, the bench, the bridge underpass).

7. **Sex and Death.** Proximity to death profoundly alters our experience of life. Write a sex scene between people who are or have recently been affected by death or the threat of death. It could be war, an illness, accident, or a natural disaster.

8. Monologues. Write a monologue in which the speaker recounts a sexual experience that ended differently from how he or she thought it would end. As always, we should know who the characters are, what they want, and what the setting has to do with the sex.

ACKNOWLEDGMENTS

I could not have put together *The Joy of Writing Sex*—the first or revised edition—without the brains, brawn, good humor, enthusiasm, and e-mail of many friends, colleagues, and near strangers who offered book titles and ideas, who listened patiently to mine, who Xeroxed stories, and lent, bought, and gave me books, in some cases with yellow Post-its jutting out like unruly bookmarks, alerting me to the exact location of the dirty parts.

Everyone I spoke to, but especially the writers who were generous enough to take time to be interviewed and who answered my letters and e-mail, helped me figure out what to tell you about how to write about sex. I am also indebted to the authors of the passages I use as examples of excellent writing. I hope their rich and varied work will be as inspiring and instructive to readers as it has been to me.

The idea for *The Joy of Writing Sex* came from the then editor in chief of Story Press, Lois Rosenthal, who called one afternoon in 1994 with an offer that, as you can see, I could not refuse. Jack Heffron, who edited the first edition, was a patient, diligent, and good-humored collaborator, who helped me to focus, organize, and get to the instructional point. Carol Houck Smith and her assistant at W. W. Norton sent me some very fine fiction that ended up in the book. Richard McCann read an early draft of the original chapter on writing about sex in the age of AIDS and guided me through it with the luminous intelligence and generosity he brings to all our encounters.

The two friends who share the dedication page died unexpectedly within thirty-six hours of each other as I was completing the first edition. Though they never met, they shared an abiding devotion to literature and to the mysterious, magical process of good writing that I hope this book honors and encourages.

For the revised edition, I have been fortunate in finding editor Elizabeth Stein, whose enthusiasm, openness, good humor, and good ideas have made writing it an endeavor that made sense and one that I knew would be treated with respect and care.

Many writers, editors, and serious readers directed me to work that ended up in this edition. I am immensely grateful to David Bergman for leading me to Andrew Holleran and to William J. Mann, and for editing the estimable *Men on Men* series of short fiction for many years; to Christopher Castellani for *Blue Angel* and much, much more; to Michael Downing; to John Jameson, the managing editor of *The Advocate*, who went above and beyond the call of duty in tracking down an article for me; to Paula Ogier, for finding one of the Internet short stories and for inviting me to give a workshop on writing fiction about sex at the Cambridge Center for Adult Education.

In finding words to express my gratitude for the inspired and conscientious work of Gail Hochman and Marianne Merola on both editions of this book, I will opt for the less-is-more approach to good writing and say simply, so that everyone can hear, thank you.

Thanks of another order are owed my breathtaking friends, from A to Z, and Emily and James, who bring music and poetry into my prose-bound life.

PERMISSIONS

Index

ABOUT THE AUTHOR

ELIZABETH BENEDICT is the author of four novels, including *Almost, The Beginner's Book of Dreams,* and *Slow Dancing,* which was a finalist for the American Book Award. Her fiction and essays have appeared in the *New York Times, Esquire, Harper's Bazaar, Salmagundi, Tin House,* the *Boston Globe,* and other publications. She is currently teaching writing at Harvard University Extension School and has taught at Princeton University, the Iowa Writers' Workshop, the New School for Social Research, and Swarthmore College. She lives in New York City and Somerville, Massachusetts.